CONTACT WITH A LORD OF KARMA

By

GEORGE KING, D.Sc., Th.D.

Printed and Published by
THE AETHERIUS SOCIETY
6202 Afton Place, Hollywood, California 90028-8298, U.S.A.

First Published — 1989

CONTACT WITH A LORD OF KARMA

COPYRIGHT OWNED BY
GEORGE KING, D.Sc., Th.D.

Copyright ©1989 by GEORGE KING

ISBN No. 0-937249-13-0
Library of Congress Catalogue Card No. 89-080234

All rights reserved. No part of this book, *Contact With A Lord Of Karma,* including all illustrations, may be reproduced or utilized in any form or by any means, electronic or mechanical, including photocopying, recording or by any information storage and retrieval system, without written permission from the Author, George King, D.Sc., Th.D.

Contact With A Lord Of Karma is printed and published by The Aetherius Society, 6202 Afton Place, Hollywood, California 90028-8298, U.S.A.

Manufactured in the United States of America.

CONTACT WITH A LORD OF KARMA
By George King, D.Sc., Th.D.

By the same Author:

THE NINE FREEDOMS
THE DAY THE GODS CAME
THE TWELVE BLESSINGS
VISIT TO THE LOGOS OF EARTH
OPERATION SPACE MAGIC — THE COSMIC CONNECTION
OPERATION SPACE POWER — The Solution to the Spiritual Energy Crisis
YOU TOO CAN HEAL
YOU ARE RESPONSIBLE!
THE THREE SAVIOURS ARE HERE!
THE FIVE TEMPLES OF GOD
THE AGE OF AETHERIUS
OPERATION SUNBEAM — GOD'S MAGIC IN ACTION
WISDOM OF THE PLANETS
LIFE ON THE PLANETS
COSMIC VOICE, VOLUME NO. 1
COSMIC VOICE, VOLUME NO. 2
KARMA AND REINCARNATION
BECOME A BUILDER OF THE NEW AGE
THIS IS THE HOUR OF TRUTH
JOIN YOUR SHIP
A COSMIC MESSAGE OF DIVINE OPPORTUNITY
MY CONTACT WITH THE GREAT WHITE BROTHERHOOD
THE FESTIVAL OF "CARRYING THE LIGHT"
DESTRUCTION OF THE TEMPLE OF DEATH and RESCUE IN SPACE
JESUS COMES AGAIN
THE HEATHER ANGEL STORY
SPACE CONTACT IN SANTA BARBARA
THE ATOMIC MISSION
A SPECIAL ASSIGNMENT
CONTACT YOUR HIGHER SELF THROUGH YOGA
BOOK OF SACRED PRAYERS
THE PRACTICES OF AETHERIUS
THE FLYING SAUCERS
THE TRUTH ABOUT DYNAMIC PRAYER
IMPORTANCE OF COMMEMORATION AND SPIRITUAL HAPPINESS
A SERIES OF LESSONS ON SPIRITUAL SCIENCE ON CASSETTES.

A price catalogue, with complete list of books and cassettes by the same Author, is available upon request.

All books and cassettes by George King, D.Sc., Th.D., are obtainable from the Publishers, The Aetherius Society, American Headquarters, 6202 Afton Place, Hollywood, California 90028-8298, U.S.A., Tel: (213) 465-9652 or 467-HEAL; or from the European Headquarters of The Aetherius Society at 757 Fulham Road, London SW6 5UU, England, Tel: (01) 736-4187 or 731-1094.

DEDICATION

This book is dedicated to The Great Lord Of Karma — Mars Sector 6 — Who is revered throughout the Galaxies.

CONTENTS

CHAPTER   PAGE

    INTRODUCTION TO THE AUTHOR 9
    INTRODUCTION 13
1   PREPARATIONS FOR THE CONTACT 17
2   A VISITATION FROM ANOTHER WORLD 23
3   CONTACT WITH A LORD OF KARMA 37
4   LATER CONTACT WITH MARS SECTOR 6 42
5   COSMIC AWARDS 49
6   AMAZING HAPPENING ON LAST HOUR
    OF SPIRITUAL PUSH 65
    CONCLUSION 75
    AUTHOR'S RECOMMENDATIONS 83

ILLUSTRATIONS

ILLUSTRATION

1   THE AUTHOR 8
2   THE HOUSE IN SANTA BARBARA 16
3   THE AUTHOR WITH CASSETTE RECORDER 21
4   THE AUTHOR'S AIDES 22
5   THE REV. RICHARD MEDWAY TESTING
    CRYSTAL WITH PENDULUM 36
6   SHREDDING THE OUTDATED DOCUMENT 48
7   DRAWING OF THE THIRD SATELLITE 64

THE AUTHOR

His Eminence Sir George King, Metropolitan Archbishop and Founder/President of The Aetherius Society; a Western Master of Yoga and an expert in astro-metaphysics, who has devoted his life in service to humanity and earned the implicit trust placed in him as Primary Terrestrial Mental Channel by The Cosmic Masters.

INTRODUCTION TO THE AUTHOR

In the world of metaphysics, or Spiritual sciences if you prefer, there has been a mass of information published dealing with many different aspects of this science. But very little has come to light which compares with the information given in this book.

This mighty step forward into the future of the Spiritual sciences has been brought about by the Author, who has dedicated an important part of his life to, not only this study, but also its application.

Born in Shropshire, England, on January 23rd, 1919, the Author took a natural interest in Religion from an early age, and even in those days, he pursued his interest with a single-minded dedication which few children of the time were able to demonstrate. Years later he was to discover why this fervent interest was inborn in him and where it was to lead him.

After World War II, he turned away from the orthodox type of Religion and practised, with the same single-mindedness, the sciences of Yoga, in which he became very proficient.

In May 1954, he was given the Command by a Master not living on this Earth to: "Prepare yourself, you are to become the voice of Interplanetary Parliament." (Note 1.)

He was later to learn that it was because of his single-mindedness and dedication to the Spiritual sciences and mankind that The Cosmic Masters had chosen him for the enormous task ahead.

He was instructed to bring into being The Aetherius Society in order to release some of the information he was about to receive. Despite all odds to the contrary in those early days of the unbelievers, he did found The Aetherius Society in London, England, in 1955.

Later, he was ordered, by The Cosmic Masters, to go to the United States of America where, in 1960, he incorporated The Aetherius Society as a Religious, scientific, educational organization.

Since the initial Contact, the Author has taken over 600 Transmissions, in a deep, Yogic Samadhic trance condition, from Masters Who are thousands of years ahead of anyone living on this Earth. He has also taken at least 400 Mental Transmissions, not in a trance state, from Cosmic Masters, right up to the present day.

He has been through many elevated experiences of a supernormal nature and has learned many things about an ancient yet modern science, which some people call "Radionics." This is the science in which subtle and psychic energies are controlled and directed. The Author performed experiments along these lines, having the burning desire to send Spiritual Healing Energies out to impoverished mankind. He succeeded in bringing about some masterful breakthroughs in this respect.

For the first time, in this modern age on the surface of Earth, prayer, healing and psychic energy could be stored in a physical container and later directed to any part of the world which was hit by a natural or man-made catastrophe.

He designed Mission after Mission himself, which were later officially accepted by The Cosmic Hierarchy of the Solar System as part of Their overall Plan for the salvation and enlightenment of mankind. He was also given assignment after assignment by The Cosmic Masters for the benefit of mankind.

Some of these feats were published and talked about on radio and television, in newspapers, magazines, periodicals, etc., mainly by others associated with the Author, and the word leaked into high places on Earth.

Honour after honour, including several Knighthoods, were bestowed upon the Author by a ruling King, an Imperial Royal Prince and Chivalric Orders alike, all of whom highly respected the Author's complete dedication to God, The Cosmic Masters and humanity.

The Author was Created and Consecrated as an Archbishop and commanded to go forth and found his own Church. Although The Aetherius Society was in operation, he nevertheless was declared as the Metropolitan Archbishop of The

Aetherius Society worldwide and uses the working title, correct by ecclesiastical and chivalric law, of — His Eminence Sir George King.

Among the distinctions, too numerous to detail here, the Author was given the high honour of Freeman of the City of London on June 12th, 1986. Of his many occupations, the authorities chose to inscribe — Author — on the official document. This is particularly significant as he has written many metaphysical books which are known throughout the world.

He was later made a member for life of the Guild of Freemen of London. He has also been elected an affiliate member of the Institute of Journalists and carries as well, two other well-known press cards.

His Eminence Sir George King has earned many doctorates, mostly of a Religious nature.

From a beginning in Shropshire, a man was born in ordinary surroundings, the son of a village schoolmaster, and from there, because of his work for mankind, gained the respect of others in authority, despite the fact that he was considered to be an unorthodox scientist. Unlike most men, who retire from active duty at the age of 65, His Eminence Sir George King has not done this but is continuing to run and build up The Aetherius Society, which now has incorporation as a Church in several different countries.

He also continues to take control of the many Missions which are solely for the benefit of the world and mankind.

Despite the fact that he has written numerous books and published well over 100 educational cassettes, he has not taken any royalties from the sale of these but instead, has insisted that the profits go to The Aetherius Society, his Church, to enable this very active organization to continue with spreading the Teachings and vitally important Work of The Cosmic Masters. The same applies to this present book, *Contact With A Lord Of Karma.*

All Material Manifestation Is a Result of the Application of Divine Mind Which Created Multitudinous Energy Fields in Which Particles of Matter Are Held in Continuous Motion.

There Is Only One Energy Crisis in the World Today — That Is, the Spiritual Energy Crisis. If This Is Put Right Within the Hearts and Minds of Mankind, Then No Other Man-Made Shortages Can Exist.

INTRODUCTION

This book — *Contact With A Lord Of Karma* — explains what happened during the mental contacts with an Elevated Cosmic Being.

The Author did make several contacts with a Being known to us for years under the title of "Mars Sector 6." (Note 2.)

During a Transmission with The Cosmic Master Aetherius on September 3rd, 1988 (Earthyear 25.58), it was revealed that because of His unselfish, single-minded devotion to helping all life streams on this Planet, as well as other inhabited worlds, Mars Sector 6 had been invited to become a Member of The Karmic Hierarchy. The Master accepted this honour.

Mars Sector 6 became a Lord Of Karma.

If you read the literature of The Aetherius Society and the Author's previously published books, study of which is absolutely essential in order to gain a deeper understanding of the Operation of Satellite No. 3, you will discover that, throughout the years, we have cooperated with the frequent terrestrial orbits of Satellite No. 3. (Note 3.) These orbits were announced previously to give us a chance to do just this.

The only contact on the physical planes of Earth between Satellite No. 3 and terrestrial man is the Author of this book, who was given the name of "Primary Terrestrial Mental Channel" in 1954. (Note 4.) This single Transmission contactee receiving the movements of Satellite No. 3 avoided confusion which would have arisen had several contacts been so chosen.

It was the Author himself who originally designed equipment capable of tuning in to Spiritual Energies from Satellite No. 3 and transmitting these Energies to mankind. (Note 5.) Not that Satellite No. 3 needed such help — but **your** Karma did, and **your** Karma and that of mankind profited greatly because of the fact that these Spiritual Energies were actually "touched" by terrestrial hands, or in other words, came through equipment designed and built on Earth.

The motive for making these telepathic contacts with The Karmic Lord Mars Sector 6, as reported in this book, was to obtain details of the future Operations of Satellite No. 3 when the Author had to leave Earth for any reason, natural causes or otherwise.

As you will read in a previous book, published in August 1987, called *Operation Space Power,* the Author and his team spent scores of hours collating information regarding the amount of Spiritual Energy which had been radiated through our Spiritual Energy Radiators throughout the years.

The results of their research and careful log keeping are staggering!

It will also amaze our readers to discover that, in the year 1988 alone, as of midnight Greenwich Mean Time, December 10th, we had transmitted **2,217,631 (two million, two hundred and seventeen thousand, six hundred and thirty-one) Prayer Hours** through our two Spiritual Energy Radiators; one in Los Angeles, California, and one in London, England. The greater portion of this Spiritual Energy came directly from Satellite No. 3 through our Spiritual Energy Radiators in a Mission we call **Operation Space Power.** (Note 6.)

In fact, to put it precisely, of this grand total — **2,148,192 (two million, one hundred and forty-eight thousand, one hundred and ninety-two) Prayer Hours came directly from Satellite No. 3 last year through our two Spiritual Energy Radiators.**

This figure does **not** include the Spiritual Energy sent out by our numerous Religious Prayer Services throughout the world, devotedly attended by our Members and sympathizers during all Spiritual Pushes.

It is little wonder that the Author, being a man completely devoted to Service to humanity, went out of his way to find out the future orbits of Satellite No. 3 so that the magnificent Operation could continue, in an uninterrupted fashion, deep into the future.

The Aetherius Society is the only Religious, scientific, educational organization on Earth which performs such a Mission.

Introduction

The uplifting, inspiring, healing Spiritual Energies which pass through both of our machines, in one year alone, must have brought immeasurable good to thousands — perhaps even millions of people on the Planet Earth.

All this in one single year!

Neither does this figure include the almost 30 years that we have been cooperating in this way with Satellite No. 3.

Information like this not only prompted the Author to find out the future orbits of Satellite No. 3, but also caused the Controller of the Satellite, Mars Sector 6, to go out of His way to be exceptionally cooperative.

When a Spiritual Master of the calibre of the Author of this book, works together in complete cooperation with a Lord Of Karma, the results are always of a positive nature!

In this book you will see for yourself the Spiritual Pushes, or orbits of Satellite No. 3 around Earth, for the next one thousand years.

That proves the understanding and trust between the Author and the Karmic Lord Mars Sector 6 — or the information would never have been given.

It also proves the complete trust that the Karmic Lord Mars Sector 6 has in the present Directors and the highly-specialized, well-trained Members of the "Special Missions Task Force" of The Aetherius Society — and those who will be elected in the future.

SPECIAL NOTE: So that the reader may understand the separate dates given in this book, the following should be remembered:

On July 8th, 1964, The Cosmic Masters, Who comprise The Spiritual Hierarchy of the Solar System, performed the most advanced astro-metaphysical Operation which had ever previously been reported to mankind — **The Primary Initiation Of Earth.** The Author was privileged to be the only channel through whom the report of this stupendous event was given to mankind and this was subsequently published in his unique book, *The Day The Gods Came.* In recognition of The Primary Initiation Of Earth, the Higher Realms and The Great White Brotherhood altered Their calendars and regarded July 8th, 1964, as Earthyear 1, Earthday 1, and continued from there.

The Author's modest home in Santa Barbara where this book was written. Several other books have been written by the Author here. This is also the house in which scores of Mental Transmissions, of vital importance to the world, have been taken.

CHAPTER 1

PREPARATIONS FOR THE CONTACT

On Tuesday, October 4th, 1988 (Earthyear 25.89), I left for Santa Barbara with the main idea of contacting Satellite No. 3 regarding the future Spiritual Push dates. (Note 7.)

It is one thing to formulate a procedure in your mind, but it is another thing to put it into operation. If the reader will stop and think, just for a moment, about the tremendous responsibility which rested on my shoulders, you will better appreciate my feelings.

The future history of the world could be affected by the answer to this question — especially due to the fact that, as the Masters had stated many years ago, Primary Terrestrial Mental Channel would NOT be replaced when he had to leave Earth.

The "Voice" would be gone.

As I stated from the public platform on Sunday, October 16th (Earthyear 25.101), I felt extremely tense about the whole situation. Admittedly, on August 18th, 1967 (Earthyear 4.42), while on the verge of the start of **Operation Karmalight**, I had been given the next Spiritual Push dates for 1,000 years. (Note 8.)

When I asked for these dates, prior to **Operation Karmalight**, had Mars Sector 6 definitely assured me, and also The Adepts, that this information would not be necessary, it is possible that greater risks would have been taken in the coming deadly Mission. As it was, The Six Adepts took as many chances of being killed or crippled in action as They dared in order to guarantee success. But had I been *refused* these dates as unnecessary, The Adepts would also have known this and They, as well as myself, would have had a different psychological outlook on Their immediate future. (Note 9.)

Win, yes — but at what cost?

The strain caused by the responsibility lying on my shoulders in those first few days of my stay in Santa Barbara impaired my health and it was only the excellent care and Healing from The Rev. Richard Medway and Brian Keneipp which brought my health back and also, with it, my confidence.

You may not realize it, but without Primary Terrestrial Mental Channel, there will be scores of unanswered questions, not only in the basic running of The Aetherius Society, **but in ALL the Cosmic Missions we perform — in fact, in ALL the Missions performed by The Great White Brotherhood and the Higher Mental Realms as well!**

No man has ever been given the "Saturn Peace Prize for Humanities," the "Venus Peace Prize for Humanities" or the "Mars Sector 6 Peace Prize for Humanities" unless these were fully deserved! (See Chapter 5.) Hence, even though I say this myself, my great importance to terrestrial life is undeniable!

Getting back to 1967, it stated on that witnessed document that the Spiritual Energy Radiators would be run every other evening during a Spiritual Push in London and Los Angeles, which meant, of course, we would halve our present operating time as these would be run on alternate evenings.

I also knew, and so do our readers, that since the old **Karma-light** days, I had been responsible for performing many Cosmic Missions and even the invention of **Operation Sunbeam** and all the equipment which went with it. (Note 10.) In themselves, these Spiritual Energy Radiators made a tremendous Karmic difference to mankind. (Note 11.)

So therefore, I had to conclude that the original information given in 1967 was now outdated, at least as far as our regular Spiritual Energy Radiator operations are concerned.

In the middle of my somewhat helpless frustration, I struck on an idea. Why not prepare a questionnaire?

You realize that, talking to a Lord Of Karma is very different from talking to your insurance agent! In fact, there are hundreds of lives difference! So I had to make sure that I did justice to the whole project.

To cut a long story short, the fax machines started working

and eventually I pulled together a questionnaire from the Tactical Teams in London and Los Angeles. (Note 12.) Oddly enough, most of the questions which were brought up, I could answer myself. However, there were one or two which I could not. So, armed with these questions, I was more prepared for the approach.

As the days went on, nearer and nearer came the end of the current Spiritual Push (i.e. September 3rd — October 9th). In the past, any communication with Satellite No. 3 should have been made during a Spiritual Push. This, too, was an added pressure.

Suddenly — a brilliant light shone through the darkness!

Without my having to contact Satellite No. 3, They contacted me with a statement that They would keep a line of communication open between myself and Themselves until the end of the next Spiritual Push, which was December 10th, 1988 (Earthyear 25.156).

I slept better that night than for many nights previously!

Another happening was confirmed by The Adepts on Thursday, October 6th (Earthyear 25.91). **I was to expect a Visitor from Satellite No. 3!**

I wanted the house empty at this time, so therefore, we booked a motel room on Saturday, October 8th, for my two assistants.

The 8th of October came and went, but not the Visitor. We did not use the motel room but had to pay for it.

We continued the booking on the 9th of October and I thought, well, this must be the last time because if the Visitor is coming from Satellite No. 3, the Vehicle goes out of orbit on October 9th.

Satellite No. 3 left orbit at 12 midnight Greenwich Mean Time (5:00 p.m. Los Angeles time) on October 9th (Earthyear 25.94) — but no Visitor!

We continued the booking through the next day, Monday the 10th of October, and the men left the house, for the motel, after serving me a nice dinner.

It was then the Visitor came.

I had already ascertained from Adept Nixies Zero Zero Five that the Visitor would not be in a physical body but that this would be a carefully-screened projection. It should be noted that any Cosmic Operator on Satellite No. 3 is extremely magnetic; in fact, so magnetic that They would not enter an ordinary house in Their Full Aspect Bodies. To do so would mean to magnetize all the clocks and weather instruments, such as barometers. The field of magnetism may even extend to the disruption of loud speaker units and the possibility of scrambling video tapes. All this, of course, without the Visitor intending to cause any damage whatsoever. Hence the projection.

It should also be pointed out that mental telepathy on this high scale is not like talking to anyone on the telephone! Anyone can speak to anyone else on the telephone, providing they both use the same language. Few people in the world are capable of the mental telepathic feats which I have demonstrated throughout the years.

In some ways, I have discovered that mental telepathy over a distance between yourself and another life stream, is not as difficult as a man-to-man approach. It is rather, in some ways, like the difference between radio and television — only not quite. In a man-to-man approach, you are liable to be distracted from your pattern of concentration by your analytical feelings of the stature, clothes worn, facial characteristics, etc., of the other; and, of course, the same applies to the Visitor. While the man-to-man approach meeting may seem easier to the uninitiated, I have found this to be incorrect.

Of course, if both are in a projected state, then both can talk quite easily to each other; but if one only is in a projected state, then exchange of information, under certain conditions, can become quite difficult.

I was prepared for this when I took up my position in the office in Santa Barbara shortly before 9:00 p.m. I put on two tape recorders: one a small hand-held; the other a portable, high-quality Sony cassette recorder. So should one fail, then the other would continue with the recording. I also had a reel-to-reel, high-quality dictaphone standing by as a back-up machine.

After making these preparations, I then, as you will read, opened up communication with Adept Nixies Zero Zero Five regarding an entirely different and personal subject.

The Author in the office of his home in Santa Barbara, holding the small cassette recorder onto which he recorded all of the Mental Transmissions appearing in this book. Close by is the second recorder, a high quality unit which is also used in the recording of all Mental Transmissions.

THE AUTHOR'S AIDES

The Author's aides, Reverend Richard Medway (left) and Brian Keneipp, both skilled craftsmen, who gave valuable assistance to the Author during both the writing of this book and many other special assignments. And, very important — Reverend Medway is also a good cook!

CHAPTER 2

A VISITATION FROM ANOTHER WORLD

His Eminence: "It is October 10th, 1988 (Earthyear 25.95), and I am now in Santa Barbara, and later on I will undoubtedly put some intelligence regarding my Visitor on this tape.

"This is (Code Name) to Nixies Zero Zero Five; please come in Nixies Zero Zero Five. (Note 13.)

"The time now is about 4 minutes before 9 o'clock p.m.

"Thank You, Nixies Zero Zero Five. Would You tell me what to do with the crystal?"

Nixies Zero Zero Five: "A little later on."

His Eminence: "Very well. Thank You, Nixies Zero Zero Five.

"I am ready to receive Whomsoever......

"A strange phenomenon happened with the lights just lately and I am expecting anybody or — any-body.

"Thank You very much, Nixies Zero Zero Five, I will wait till 9:00 p.m. The time now is just a minute or two away from that.

"Nixies Zero Zero Five, would You please forgive me if I seem to be a trifle nervous?"

Nixies Zero Zero Five: "I will forgive you."

His Eminence: "Thank You. This is (Code Name) standing by."

Nixies Zero Zero Nine: "Can you feel Me?"

His Eminence: "Yes I can. Welcome to my little house in Santa Barbara. This is only a small dwelling really, but may I conduct You, later on, around our Headquarters in Los Angeles, which is one of the Headquarters we have?

"First of all, Sir, I know that You are Nixies Zero Zero Nine."

Nixies Zero Zero Nine: "You are right about that."

His Eminence: "Sir, may I invite You into my office. It is not very much of an office, I must admit; however, it is my office for the time being.

"May I record You — or at least, what You say?"

Nixies Zero Zero Nine: "I am Nixies Zero Zero Nine Who played a part in 'Gilbert'." (Note 14.)

His Eminence: "Yes, I know that."

Nixies Zero Zero Nine: "It is true what The Master Aetherius said many years ago, that The Three Adepts would not be replaced when They were requested to leave the Planet Earth. However, since that time, there have been Cosmic manipulations and The Five Adepts will be replaced by Nixies Zero Zero Six, Nixies Zero Zero Seven, Nixies Zero Zero Eight and Nixies Zero Zero Nine, but not in terrestrial bodies. (Note 15.)

His Eminence: "Well, thank You very much, I think we all will agree that is absolutely fabulous!"

Nixies Zero Zero Nine: "I apologize for not visiting you before now because I had to take Satellite No. 3 out of orbit and land it on Jupiter 4."

His Eminence: "Really! Well, it looks as though You and the other two Chaps are pretty hot Pilots!"

Nixies Zero Zero Nine: "I am talking to one now!"

His Eminence: "Sir, it is rather warm this evening, may I take my jacket and tie off and put on my air conditioning system?"

Nixies Zero Zero Nine: "Yes, you may."

His Eminence: "Thank You very much for agreeing with that.

(pause)

"I have not put on the air conditioning system but I have been around the place and I have opened some windows.

"With Your permission, may I take You around my small dwelling?"

Nixies Zero Zero Nine: "Yes please."

His Eminence: "Thank You.

"We will start in the kitchen area, which I assume You are familiar with. This is the kitchen area You see, small but adequate for the size of this dwelling; and this is the main dining room-cum-lounge area. We have television and hi-fi — that type of stuff, which is fairly good as far as it goes. We have two video tape players here."

Nixies Zero Zero Nine: "I am interested in small dwellings like this."

His Eminence: "Thank You. We have a bedroom here with, of course, facilities of a toilet and shower — Earth people have to shower themselves; and we have a small guest room here. Oh yes, this is a computer and a printout section. The people who work this are not here tonight."

Nixies Zero Zero Nine: "I am sorry they are not here."

His Eminence: "I apologize to You, Sir, for sending them into a hotel tonight."

Nixies Zero Zero Nine: "That was not necessary."

His Eminence: "Necessary or not, Sir, I am afraid I probably made that mistake."

Nixies Zero Zero Nine: "(Code Name) cannot make such a mistake!"

His Eminence: "(Code Name) is very prone to making mistakes!

"This is my bedroom and so on."

Nixies Zero Zero Nine: "What about the table here?"

His Eminence: "There are one or two emergency medicines there — mostly water; and, of course, the usual facilities here.

"This is my office. Yes, that is a facsimile machine. We have a fax here and one in Los Angeles and one in England."

Nixies Zero Zero Nine: "I would like to see how the fax works."

His Eminence: "Very well. I am closed off from phone calls now but I will ask Los Angeles to send You a fax — with Your permission."

I then left the office and made a phone call to the American Headquarters in Los Angeles. I contacted Dr. Charles Abrahamson and asked him to send me a quick fax. He was surprised to receive this request because I had already previously told Los Angeles and London that no communications were to come through to me unless they were vitally urgent.

I went back into the office again, where my visitor remained, and told Him that the fax would be received shortly. I also showed Him other fax messages which we had received just lately, one of which asked for particulars of **Operation Sunbeam** — number of Phases and location, etc. He examined these with great care.

I explained to Him that on some of the facsimiles we send from Santa Barbara, we ask for a receipt and understanding from the receiver and I showed him a fax bearing these words.

We then started up conversation again.

His Eminence: "In the meantime, Sir, may I talk about other things?"

Nixies Zero Zero Nine: "Yes, you may. You like tea?"

His Eminence: "Yes, I do like tea."

Nixies Zero Zero Nine: "Would you please show Me how tea is made?"

His Eminence: "We have to go to the kitchen for that, Sir."

Nixies Zero Zero Nine: "Very well."

The projected thought-form of Nixies Zero Zero Nine followed me into the kitchen and I explained to Him that you turn on the gas and put some water on the stove, heat it and then pour it over a teabag, later adding milk and sugar — and there you have one cup of tea, all of which He seemed very interested in.

His Eminence: "Have You ever seen tea made before?"

Nixies Zero Zero Nine: "I have not."

His Eminence: "Very well then, Sir, it is a very simple procedure. Any Man Who can move the Satellite out of orbit and dock it on Jupiter 4 must be a rather skilled Operative — and yet You state that You have never seen tea made? Very well, Sir, I will make some for You.

"You see, you pour the boiling water over the teabag and duck it like so. As far as I am concerned, I like mild tea, so I only have the teabag ducked a few times then I put it away. Now to the refrigerator to pull out the cream which I like in the tea."

Nixies Zero Zero Nine: "Do all people like cream in their tea?"

His Eminence: "No, not all people, but I for one do, so I pour the cream in the tea like that, which is fairly obvious.

"Now, You see, I am different — I like cool tea. Very well. So all I do to cool this stuff down is to pour a little water in like that."

Nixies Zero Zero Nine: "Why did you not use the main tap?"

His Eminence: "That is because the water I used comes through a filter."

Nixies Zero Zero Nine: "May I see it?"

His Eminence: "Yes Sir. *(I then opened the door beneath the sink.)*

"See? That is a filter which clears a lot of the particles out of the water, including most of the chemicals they put in the water in order to purify it."

Nixies Zero Zero Nine: "May I examine some filtered water and some water from the tap?"

I used two clean glasses; one containing ordinary tap water and one containing filtered water. I held these up so that my Visitor could examine them.

His Eminence: "Very well, Sir. This is our filtered water —

that is the water from the tap."

Nixies Zero Zero Nine: "There is no comparison. That (the tap water) should be thrown away or only used for other chores. This (the filtered water) can be drunk." *(He obviously used His E.S.P. in this analysis.)*

His Eminence: "Yes, that is why I have the filter on the tap. Right?

"As You are not in a physical body at the moment and therefore You cannot drink it, I will take my tea with me if I may."

Nixies Zero Zero Nine: "May I see this fax come through?"

His Eminence: "If my people in Los Angeles are quick — ah, there it is. Now You see, here we have a fax transmission which was sent from Los Angeles. The same thing could have been sent from — London even, and it is what I requested:

"*'Good luck, Master, from all of us. Charles Abrahamson.'*

"That is how a basic terrestrial fax machine works."

Nixies Zero Zero Nine: "Thank you."

His Eminence: "If I may sip my tea. I am trying to run two recorders at the same time, Sir. That is the fax transmission we have received, since I requested it on the telephone. It says: *'Good luck, Master, from all of us,'* signed by Charles Abrahamson."

I held up the fax transmission and read it again. Nixies Zero Zero Nine duly scanned the whole process and possibly transmitted the result of His mental scan of the fax message.

His Eminence: "Now, what else can we show You?"

Nixies Zero Zero Nine: "Can you send back an answer to that?"

His Eminence: "Oh yes, but I am sure You do not require that?"

Nixies Zero Zero Nine: "I do not."

His Eminence: "Thank You."

Nixies Zero Zero Nine: "Is that a quartz crystal?"

His Eminence: "Yes, and Nixies Zero Zero Five was going to request that I put that out tonight on a table on the lawn and The Adepts were going to Charge it."

Nixies Zero Zero Nine: "I request you to put it out there now."

His Eminence: "Very well, I will."

I then took the crystal from the office and placed it upon a wooden table, which I had previously arranged on the lawn in a position which was clear of overhanging branches of bushes. I then returned to the office.

Nixies Zero Zero Nine: "I will relay a message to The Adepts about that."

His Eminence: "Yes. This is (Code Name) to Nixies Zero Zero Five.

"Our good Friend here, Nixies Zero Zero Nine, is going to relay a message — or already has done."

Nixies Zero Zero Five: "We are now proceeding to Charge the crystal as We intended to do."

His Eminence: "Thank You very much indeed."

The quartz crystal mentioned was one that I had mounted in a wooden base some years ago. As a matter of fact, most of the time it stayed up in Santa Barbara and it was only recently I took it back to Los Angeles and Charged it myself. However, because of certain happenings, I had previously asked The Adepts to discharge the crystal and clear it of all influences — which They had done already. As you have read, They did alert me during the Contact with Nixies Zero Zero Nine and asked me to put the quartz crystal out on a table in the garden.

His Eminence: "I am very indebted to You People — and indebted to You, Nixies Zero Zero Nine; after all, You did do a little bit in the 'Gilbert' Operation, did You not?"

Nixies Zero Zero Nine: "I would have taken it down."

His Eminence: "I know. You would have taken it down — yes, I know. However, You have to become used to the Karmic complexities of Terra. I am afraid You do — Old Boy! (Note 16)

"However, it appears that You, Nixies Zero Zero Seven and Nixies Zero Zero Eight — not in any way to discount Nixies Zero Zero Six — are intending to remain in close contact with Earth, even when The Five Adepts have to leave."

Nixies Zero Zero Nine: "That is quite correct and I feel very inadequate."

His Eminence: "Who is appointed as the Chief Communicator?"

Nixies Zero Zero Nine: "I am classed as the Chief Communications Agent. I feel extremely inadequate and I intend to take what educational courses are available."

His Eminence: "Very well. Have You yet received Your Diploma in Terrestrial Psychology?"

Nixies Zero Zero Nine: "I have a Diploma in Terrestrial Psychology which is valid up to your year 2020. Also, you received yours in the terrestrial year 1870."

His Eminence: "I do not exactly remember it in my physical body at the moment, but I am sure I did — yes, I did, because You have seen the document. Thank You, I like the idea of that.

"Thank You, Sir."

The educational courses referred to by Adept Nixies Zero Zero Nine are specially-run computer imprint educational courses — as far as He is concerned, possibly on Satellite No. 3. The applicant is first closely mentally scanned to see whether or not He can withstand the pressures exerted during what may be termed as an "educational course." If He is willing and able mentally to absorb high-speed information, He is then taught a particular subject by computer.

As Nixies Zero Zero Nine stated, He received a Diploma in

Terrestrial Psychology which is valid up to the year 2020, and He also saw my Diploma in Terrestrial Psychology, which educational course was given in the year 1870 — before I was born in this present life. This Diploma would also be valid into the future because They would have predicted the advancement in terrestrial psychological research and have made allowances for this. So, because mine was received in the year 1870 does not mean to say that the teaching only applied to the terrestrial advancement of that year.

It becomes necessary for any Cosmic Adept, working very closely with terrestrials, to be educated in terrestrial ways. It must have been foreseen, even in the year 1870, that I would personally have to play a very important role in terrestrial affairs, as well as Cosmic affairs. It was probably even foreseen then, that the person who would be born in the next life as George King would also become Primary Terrestrial Mental Channel.

A truly frightening concept — yet a truly great one! But that is another long story!

Nixies Zero Zero Nine: "I cannot understand why you call Me 'Sir'."

His Eminence: "It is out of deference.

"You came to introduce Yourself to me as one of The Adepts Who would take the place of The Five Adepts when They leave Earth. I am extremely indebted to You for this action."

Nixies Zero Zero Nine: *(Comment unrecorded.)*

His Eminence: "Yes, well, I have lived on Earth for a few years, have I not? Very well, we will talk about that privately, will we not?

"Thank You."

After a private conversation, we came down to a fact which was very interesting. Nixies Zero Zero Nine has had first-hand experience on Satellite No. 3 in many different Magnetization Orbits, not only of this Earth but through other Systems as well; and also He tells me that He has had some experience with Space combat, but He tells me that His cannot be compared to the experience of The Three Adepts and/or The Five Adepts. I do not know what answer I can give to that, except to say — **They were there when They were needed.**

His Eminence: "This is (Code Name) to Nixies Zero Zero Five. Thank You very much, Nixies Zero Zero Five."

Nixies Zero Zero Five: "The crystal has been partially Charged with as much Energy as We should put into it at this present time."

His Eminence: "Thank You very much, Nixies Zero Zero Five.

"With deference to You, Nixies Zero Zero Nine, may I retrieve the crystal?"

Nixies Zero Zero Nine: "You may."

His Eminence: "Thank You."

I retrieved the crystal and put it back on my desk.

His Eminence: "This is (Code Name) to Nixies Zero Zero Five. I am not going to ask You how I use this because I already know, but are there any limitations?"

Nixies Zero Zero Five: "One limitation — you should not lend it to anyone else because the Power would not be acceptable by them."

His Eminence: "Thank You very much. Is the frequency high then? *(pause)* All right, we go to silence!

"Thank You, Nixies Zero Zero Five, I have received that information and we have our Friend here, Nixies Zero Zero Nine, Who has — out of respect for me, which I take as a great compliment — introduced Himself to me at this time.

"Yes, Nixies Zero Zero Nine, You will look around the Los Angeles Headquarters I hope."

Nixies Zero Zero Nine: "I have already taken a partial scan of the operation but I would not go any further than that without your permission."

His Eminence: "Thank You. May I show You around when I arrive back in Los Angeles? I am leaving here on Wednesday — any time after that?"

Nixies Zero Zero Nine: "I wish to thank you for that."

His Eminence: "And I thank You very much.

"Now, may I please sum up what You have said?"

Nixies Zero Zero Nine: "Yes, you may."

His Eminence: "Your main Mission here was to introduce Yourself to me. Also, You stated that when The Five Adepts have to leave the Planet Earth, You and Your Colleagues will remain; that You will be the Chief Communications Officer when The Adepts have gone; that You will receive all communications regarding Missions from my colleagues here, Aetherius Society Tactical Team Members; however, You cannot guarantee to reply to them. But I am sure they will be relieved to know that You are monitoring them."

Nixies Zero Zero Nine: "I will monitor them."

His Eminence: "Now, The Masters from Gotha, as You know, perform the Spiritual Energy release in **Operation Sunbeam** and They intend to stay because **Operation Sunbeam** will be performed in the future." (Note 17.)

Nixies Zero Zero Nine: "I think that is a brilliant idea and I will leave that Mission to Them. However, I will be available for further communications with you in the near future."

His Eminence: "Thank You very much, Nixies Zero Zero Nine. Thank You for coming to visit me and to introduce Yourself to me and look around my small domicile in Santa Barbara, and I will look forward, in the future, to showing You around my Headquarters in Los Angeles."

Nixies Zero Zero Nine: "I wish to thank you for that. I will look forward to this privilege and will make arrangements for that."

His Eminence: "Thank You very much.

"This is (Code Name) ending Communique for the time being with Nixies Zero Zero Nine.

"The time now is 9:45 p.m., Santa Barbara."

After this very interesting visit, Adept Nixies Zero Zero Nine left.

He proved to be very perceptive, especially since He was not used to visiting small terrestrial houses. For one thing, among many others, He noticed immediately that I cooled down my tea with water from a smaller tap than the main one. In fact, He was so interested in this, as you have read, that He asked to see the filter. I did open the door under the sink to show Him the filter but really do not believe I needed to do that. Thinking back on the experience, I feel He could easily have seen through the door!

The fact that He gave an immediate opinion of the comparison between ordinary tap water, which He considered to be "undrinkable," and filtered water, which He considered to be "drinkable," proves that He had deep perceptive powers.

Let us not forget, here was a closely-screened projection and at no time did He display a fraction of His real power and ability.

I was informed by Cosmic Sources during the last Stand-By on Lake Powell, between 5:00 p.m. — 8:00 a.m. on April 28th/29th, 1988 (Earthyear 24.296/297), that three more Adepts were Karmically allowed to supplement the existing Force of six, but I was told to keep this information secret until it was later partially released.

I was not surprised during the "Gilbert" Operation when Adepts Nixies Zero Zero Seven, Nixies Zero Zero Eight and Nixies Zero Zero Nine joined, with Adepts Nixies Zero Zero Four and Nixies Zero Zero Five, in the Spiritual Energy manipulation. As a matter of fact, Nixies Zero Zero Eight and Nixies Zero Zero Nine first came as observers and I remember thinking at the time, I wonder how long They will be observing? (Note 14.)

After meeting Nixies Zero Zero Nine I knew why my suspicions were well founded.

It was not long before They were both in action. Neither was it by chance that hurricane "Gilbert" did not vere off towards Texas, which all the experts said it was due to do. Neither was it by chance that the whole hurricane lost a tremendous amount of its power — against all expert opinion. It is true that Adepts Nixies Zero Zero Eight and Nixies Zero Zero Nine did play: "**A little part in the 'Gilbert' Mission.**"

I feel sure that we will hear more about Nixies Zero Zero Nine and the other Two as time goes on.

After my Visitor left, and after I had time to compose myself a little, I rang up the motel and asked Richard and Brian to return to the house, which they did. Both Richard and Brian were very excited when I told them what had happened between myself and Nixies Zero Zero Nine. I did not give them the story in full, as by then it was becoming late and I was tired. However, I did also tell them about the crystal being Charged by Adepts Nixies Zero Zero Four and Nixies Zero Zero Five. Although there was only supposed to be a partial Charge in this crystal, however, when measured by the pendulum, the Charge seemed to be very considerable, as far as we were concerned. The Spiritual Energy seemed to leave the apex of the crystal in an upward spiral which had an effect on the pendulum for over two feet above the top of the crystal. I actually used some of the Spiritual Energy from it before I went to bed that night.

Although the meeting between myself and Nixies Zero Zero Nine had been extremely pleasant, however, this was not why I had made the trip to Santa Barbara and retired that night determined that the next day, Tuesday, October 11th, I would attempt to contact Satellite No. 3 about the future Spiritual Push dates.

I arose the following morning, after only a partial night of sleep, and then went for a walk along the cliffs. After this, I ate a light lunch and went for a rest and some massage to take out the excessive tension in my shoulders.

One thing the visit from Nixies Zero Zero Nine had done, among other things, was to give me back my confidence so that I was better able to shoulder the immense responsibility which rested upon me. The rest you will read on the following pages.

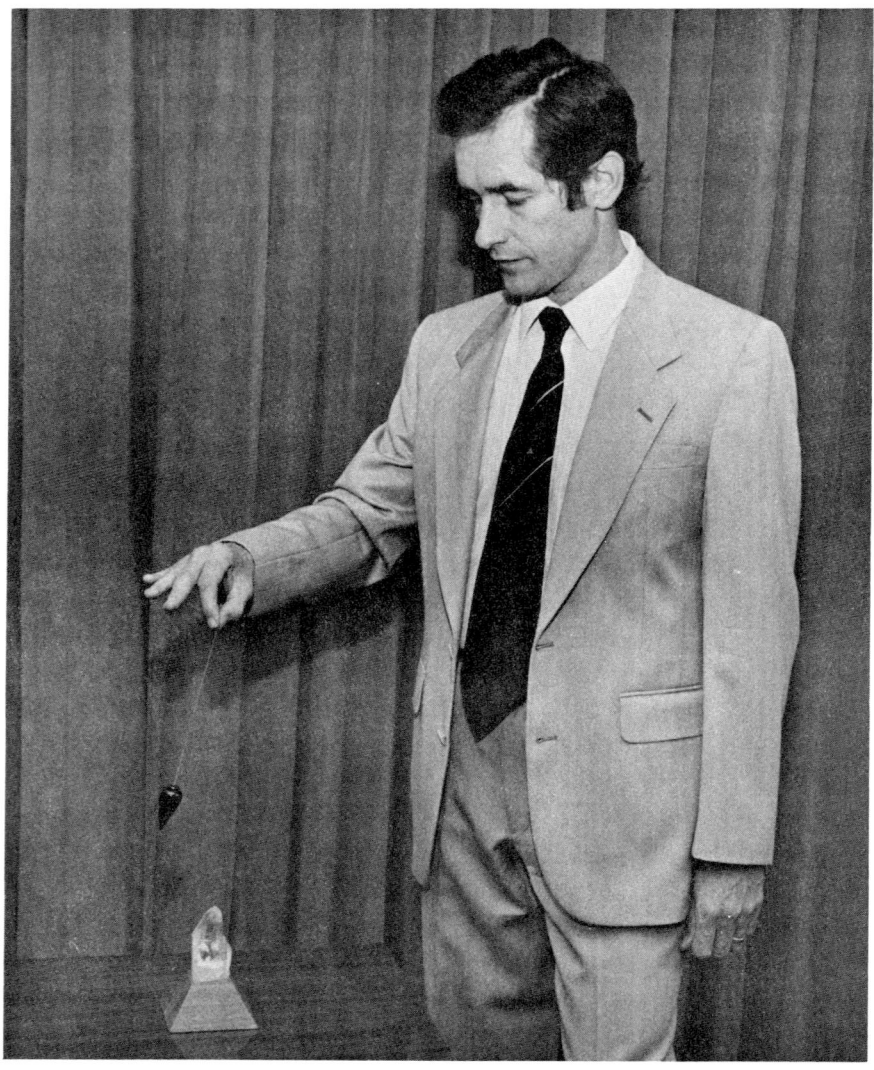

Reverend Richard Medway uses his expertise with the pendulum to measure the direction of the radiation of Spiritual Energy from the Author's crystal, which The Adepts had just partially Charged for his own use. The result indicated that the power was very considerable.

CHAPTER 3

CONTACT WITH A LORD OF KARMA

"FUTURE SPIRITUAL PUSH DATES"

His Eminence: "It is October 11th, 1988 (Earthyear 25.96). I am in Santa Barbara. The time now is 3:15 p.m. and I am making an attempt to communicate with Satellite No. 3.

"This is (Code Name) to Satellite No. 3; (Code Name) to Satellite No. 3 under Emergency Code...... (Code Name) to Satellite No. 3 under Emergency Code......

"Satellite No. 3 is, at the moment, on Jupiter 4.

"Thank You very much, Satellite No. 3. I would like to communicate about the future 'Magnetization Period' dates if I may.

"Yes, Satellite No. 3, I am breaking this into two distinct phases. At the present time, I will deal with the dates, if that is possible, and two questions. Then I am going to discuss other questions which I will need to pose at a later time."

Mars Sector 6: "This is Mars Sector 6."

His Eminence: "This is (Code Name) to Mars Sector 6. Thank You, Mars Sector 6.

"Are You prepared, at this particular time, to give a future forecast for the 'Magnetization Period' dates when The Adepts may have to leave Earth, or when I have to leave Earth?"

Mars Sector 6: "I am so prepared."

His Eminence: "Thank You, Mars Sector 6. *(pause)* Yes, I will do that for a matter of record. The 1988 'Magnetization Period' dates were:

> March 7th to March 12th — Emergency Period.
> April 18th to May 23rd.

July 5th to August 5th.
September 3rd to October 9th.
November 4th to December 10th."

Mars Sector 6: "These dates will stand. There will not be an alteration in these dates, with the exception of the following......"

His Eminence: "I am pulling the information which was given on the 18th of August in the year 1967. That document was signed by three witnesses, who witnessed my signature, and also it had a Notary Seal on it. So this earlier one is no longer valid?"

Mars Sector 6: "That is no longer valid.

"Now the exception. These dates will be logged as from 1989 and there will be one major exception, and that is this: the dates of the Emergency Periods may vary slightly and then they will be fixed."

His Eminence: "When will they vary slightly?"

Mars Sector 6: "I will give you further information regarding that. **The rest of the dates are fixed for as long as it is possible for The Aetherius Society to cooperate with them.**"

His Eminence: "Thank You very much. So I will communicate further with You at a later time regarding these Emergency Periods — I take it there will be some?"

Mars Sector 6: "Yes, there will be Emergency Periods."

His Eminence: "Are You going to break the whole project up into cycles as You did last time, such as: the First Cycle — 250 years; the Second Cycle — 500 years; the Third Cycle — 150 years; the Fourth Cycle — 100 years?"

Mars Sector 6: "I do not think that this is necessary or even advisable at this time."

His Eminence: "Very well. Then these dates, apart from the Emergency Periods which will be given at a later time, are fixed for as long as it is possible for us to cooperate with them. Thank You very much.

"Now, question: Should both Spiritual Energy Radiators continue to operate from 8:00 p.m. to 11:00 p.m. local time, during each Spiritual Push?"

Mars Sector 6: "Yes."

His Eminence: "Should the London Headquarters operate their Spiritual Energy Radiator for the **last four hours,** ending at 12 midnight G.M.T. on the last day of each Spiritual Push?"

Mars Sector 6: "Yes."

His Eminence: "Thank You.

"I think that is all I have in the first phase of these questions. Phase two will be a little more complex."

Mars Sector 6: "You can bring up phase two after the discussion already spoken about."

His Eminence: "Very well — what do I call You?"

Mars Sector 6: "Mars Sector 6." (Note 18.)

His Eminence: "Very well, Mars Sector 6, thank You very much."

Mars Sector 6: "Inform those concerned that The Adepts Nixies Zero Zero Four and Nixies Zero Zero Five will leave Terra **after** The Three Adepts."

His Eminence: "After The Three Adepts have left, we will have quite a line-up of Adepts — Nixies Zero Zero Four, Nixies Zero Zero Five, Nixies Zero Zero Six, Nixies Zero Zero Seven, Nixies Zero Zero Eight and Nixies Zero Zero Nine.

"Nixies Zero Zero Four and Nixies Zero Zero Five will probably stay on for some months **after** the last of The Three Adepts have left and then, of course, Nixies Zero Zero Six will be here all the time, and Nixies Zero Zero Seven, Nixies Zero Zero Eight and Nixies Zero Zero Nine will be here all the time as well. **Well, it looks as though mankind is having a full line of protection here.**"

"So, will Nixies Zero Zero Four and Nixies Zero Zero Five leave after The Adepts — when They are able to?"

Mars Sector 6: "They will. They will stay here until it is safe for Them to leave Terra."

His Eminence: "Well, that is very good news. I am sure everybody will be very happy about that."

Mars Sector 6: "I advise you, in this discussion, not to try and foresee every little thing which may possibly happen. Even though the 'Voice' will be gone, as far as possible, the cooperation with Satellite No. 3 will be as you have performed it in the past."

His Eminence: "Thank You. I honestly believe that this is all the information I need at the present time.

"May I ask either Your worthy Self or one of Your Colleagues to scan the tape when I replay?"

Mars Sector 6: "You may do this."

His Eminence: "Thank You."

I then wound back one cassette tape and replayed the message in full.

His Eminence: "I have replayed the tape. The time now is 3:45 p.m. This is (Code Name).

"Oh, Mars Sector 6 — **You** scanned the tape?"

Mars Sector 6: "Yes, I did. I fully agree with everything on that tape and if any more questions do arise when others hear it, you may bring them to Me."

His Eminence: "Very well, and I will be bringing to You a question about the Emergency Periods when possible. Thank You."

Mars Sector 6: "This is Mars Sector 6 from Satellite No. 3 now on Jupiter 4."

His Eminence: "This is (Code Name) now in Santa Barbara on Planet Earth.

"This is the termination of our present Communique."

After the last Transmission from The Cosmic Lord, we left Los Angeles on October 30th/31st, 1988 (Earthyear 25.115/116), with an elite Team to perform another Cosmic Mission called **The Saturn Mission,** over a Psychic Centre of Earth in Utah. (Note 19.) On the way back from successfully accomplishing this Mission, we were held up by fierce storms. However, everybody did arrive safely back at the American Headquarters in Los Angeles on November 16th, 1988 (Earthyear 25.132).

Despite the fact that I had accomplished Phase 22 of **The Saturn Mission,** under occasionally very difficult conditions, I would not allow myself to rest too long because I left Los Angeles with The Rev. Richard Medway and Brian Keneipp on November 18th (Earthyear 25.134).

I was eager to have the problem of the Emergency Periods solved.

My house in Santa Barbara gave me peace and quiet so that this vitally important line of communication with Mars Sector 6 could be re-opened and, as you can read, this was successfully accomplished and the information given.

THE SPIRITUAL PUSH DATES FOR THE FUTURE WILL BE:
(from 1989 onwards)

April 18th to May 23rd (inclusive).
July 5th to August 5th (inclusive).
September 3rd to October 9th (inclusive).
November 4th to December 10th (inclusive).

Special Note 1: It should be noted, as already stated in the Introduction, that these dates are given for the next 1,000 terrene years. This applies whether or not The Aetherius Society is able to cooperate with them for this long. As Mars Sector 6 stated, the Spiritual Energies radiated to Earth from Satellite No. 3 are for the benefit of **all** life streams on the Planet.

Special Note 2: For information regarding the changing Emergency Periods, please read the next Chapter.

CHAPTER 4

LATER CONTACT WITH MARS SECTOR 6

His Eminence: "The date is November 20th, 1988 (Earthyear 25.136). My position is Santa Barbara. The time now is just before 10:35 a.m.

"This is (Code Name) to Satellite No. 3; (Code Name) to Satellite No. 3. Come in Satellite No. 3 under Special Code...."

"Thank You, Satellite No. 3. The time now is just before 10:40 a.m."

Mars Sector 6: "This is Mars Sector 6 from Satellite No. 3, now in Magnetization Orbit Terra. Regarding the Emergency Periods:

"While Primary Terrestrial Mental Channel is still alive on this Planet, you will continue as normal, with information given at the beginning of each year, as it has been in the past.

"However, after due consultation, We have decided **not** to include the dates of the Emergency Periods in the future forecast as this would provide too many complications for those people who are left when Primary Terrestrial Mental Channel has to leave Earth.

"There will be Emergency Periods. These will vary from year to year, but We will look after them Ourselves with a manipulation of Spiritual Energy from Satellite No. 3, through either The Adepts or certain aspects of what you call — The Great White Brotherhood. (Note 20.)

"This is Mars Sector 6. Do you understand that?"

His Eminence: "Yes, I understand that very well. I have, as You telepathed it, put the information on two tape recorders and there can be no confusion about the information.

"Mars Sector 6, from Primary Terrestrial Mental Channel: Do I have permission, at this time, to ask one or two questions?"

Mars Sector 6: "You have that permission."

His Eminence: "Thank You. I will read the questions if I may.

"Question No. 1: In the event of a severe natural catastrophe or political upheaval requiring a Spiritual Energy Radiator to be moved to another location, is there anywhere on Earth that we should **not** move to for magnetic or geophysical reasons?"

Mars Sector 6: "As far as I can see, **no** — but every case has to be judged on its own merit. With certain changes on the surface of the Planet Earth, those people left in control will have to use their own initiative as to what place may be considered safe for geophysical reasons, but not necessarily for magnetic reasons. The Spiritual Energy Radiator will still operate, even in heavy natural magnetic fields."

His Eminence: "Thank You very much.

"Question No. 2: Is there an optimum number of Spiritual Energy Radiators which can be built for cooperation with Satellite No. 3?"

Mars Sector 6: "The answer to this question is **no, providing they are all under the strict control of The Aetherius Society.**"

His Eminence: "Thank You.

"Question No. 3: Is it permissible to run two or more Spiritual Energy Radiators concurrently, in the same time zone, other than during the first and last hours of a Spiritual Push; or should we run one at a different time, other than 8:00 p.m. to 11:00 p.m.?"

Mars Sector 6: "The answer to this question is **yes,** you should. If they are both in the same time zone, then one ideally should be run in the morning and one run at the normal time, 8:00 p.m. to 11:00 p.m."

His Eminence: "Thank You.

"Question No. 4: In the event of **Operation Prayer Power** discharges, such as the recent hurricane 'Gilbert,' where it was coordinated with Satellite No. 3, is there a procedure we should follow in the future? (Note 21.) In emergency situations, would it be possible for **Operation Space Power II** stored Energies to be sent through our Spiritual Energy Radiators?" (Note 22.)

Mars Sector 6: "With the 'Voice' gone, that could present some complications. I would suggest that this subject be discussed with your Operators and a certain line of approach be formulated and then put to Me for My consideration."

His Eminence: "Thank You very much. I do believe that You have put the whole situation in a nutshell, I may say, and thank You for doing so.

"May I, with Your permission please, wind back this tape so that the information can be monitored by one of Your Colleagues to make sure that there is nothing on the tape which is incorrect?"

Mars Sector 6: "You may do that."

His Eminence: "Thank You."

I wound back the cassette on one tape recorder and re-played it.

His Eminence: "This is (Code Name) to Satellite No. 3. Do You agree with what is on that tape?"

Mars Sector 6: "I agree with what is on that tape."

His Eminence: "Thank You very much. We will discuss question number 4 and we will work out a line of approach which will be surrendered to You as soon as this has been done.

"Oh, I am communicating with Mars Sector 6! Thank You very much, Mars Sector 6 — **You** monitored the tape?"

Mars Sector 6: "Yes, I did."

His Eminence: "Very well. One more question if I may. May I publish the whole of Your last Mental Transmission on the Spiritual Push dates — and this one?"

Mars Sector 6: "Yes, that would be a good idea. When this is published, you have to make it clear that this is concerned with Spiritual Energy Radiator operation **under strict Aetherius Society control,** even though Satellite No. 3 does orbit Terra to help anyone on Earth, irrespective of race, colour, class or creed."

His Eminence: "Thank You, yes, I will make that plain and clear. The publication will appear in a small book and there will be no confusion at all, throughout the years, as to what was said and what was not said."

"This is Primary Terrestrial Mental Channel closing down communication for the time being with Mars Sector 6 regarding the Emergency Periods and certain posed questions."

Mars Sector 6: "This is Mars Sector 6 from Satellite No. 3, now in Magnetization Orbit Terra, closing down communication for the present time with Primary Terrestrial Mental Channel."

His Eminence: "This is Primary Terrestrial Mental Channel to Mars Sector 6. Thank You very much for that. I am overjoyed and deeply relieved to receive this information, I can tell You!"

Mars Sector 6: "I say to you personally — Go with God."

His Eminence: "And I return the Blessing.

"End of communication.

"Time now is 11:00 a.m., Sunday, November 20th, 1988 (Earthyear 25.136), Santa Barbara."

While he is living on Earth, His Eminence Sir George King is the only person designated by The Cosmic Masters as "Primary Terrestrial Mental Channel," through whom specific information, such as the annual "Magnetization Periods," is relayed to mankind. By maintaining only **one** channel for this information, possible confusion is avoided by anyone else "claiming" to receive conflicting information.

The Cosmic Masters have decided to avoid such danger of confusion in the future also, so that when Primary Terrestrial Mental Channel has to leave Earth, those remaining will not be put in the position of having to determine the legitimacy of information which is believed or "claimed" to be received from Higher Forces, relating to such vitally important matters as the operation of Satellite No. 3 during Emergency Periods.

In the text, which we repeat for emphasis, Mars Sector 6 had this to say:

"However, after due consultation, We have decided not to include the dates of the Emergency Periods in the future forecast as this would provide too many complications for those people who are left when Primary Terrestrial Mental Channel has to leave Earth."

This statement avoids all complications regarding the Emergency Periods in the future when Primary Terrestrial Mental Channel has to leave the Planet Earth.

It also does something else of great importance. It leaves Satellite No. 3 free to operate at any time They are allowed by Karmic Law to make an Emergency Magnetization Orbit of Terra. Had They made any attempt to give us particulars of the Emergency Periods, as you can see, this would have imposed a limitation on the operation of the Satellite during these varying periods. Unlike the actual main Spiritual Push dates, which are now fixed and will not vary, the Emergency Periods will vary.

The Author feels that readers will agree with him that this is a brilliant strategic move made by Mars Sector 6 and other Cosmic Masters.

There was in this mental communication with Mars Sector 6 another question of great importance which I brought up. This was question number 4. As you can read, Mars Sector 6 suggested we hold further discussions on this question because, with the "Voice" gone, it was liable to pose some problems and I think He wanted to find out exactly how far the Tactical Team Members were able to go.

To repeat this question for emphasis because of its vast importance, it is this:

In the event of Operation Prayer Power situation discharges, such as the recent hurricane "Gilbert," where it was coordinated

with Satellite No. 3, is there a procedure we should follow in the future? In emergency situations, would it be possible for Operation Space Power II stored Energies to be sent through our Spiritual Energy Radiators?

On Wednesday, November 23rd, 1988 (Earthyear 25.139), I went back to the American Headquarters in Los Angeles, together with my aides, and on Thursday, November 24th (Earthyear 25.140), Thanksgiving Day, we had a meeting regarding this question with the Tactical Team Members in Los Angeles and we put together a Modus Operandi.

I would like to state here that this was one of the most successful meetings we have ever had. If those Tactical Team Members present did nothing else in celebration of the national American holiday Thanksgiving, they certainly celebrated it far more importantly than any other people in the United States.

Some very fine ideas were brought up and a correct Modus Operandi worked out for this procedure which, you will admit, was a difficult one, especially, as Mars Sector 6 says, with the "Voice" gone.

Soon after this, I left for Santa Barbara again and contacted Mars Sector 6 on November 30th, 1988 (Earthyear 25.146), starting at 10:20 a.m. and ending after 11:00 a.m.

Mars Sector 6 put His stamp of approval and agreement on our proposed Modus Operandi and gave instructions that we should practise this. He also agreed with me that this ritual should **not** be published and it should involve just a **few carefully chosen Tactical Team Members in The Aetherius Society.**

After this, the Great Karmic Lord also suggested to me that I could contact Him further with any questions which may arise from the practice of this simple but very powerful ritual, which I promised to do.

I must say, during the communications with Mars Sector 6 regarding the Spiritual Push dates, Emergency Periods and so on, for the future, He was **more than helpful** to me and **more than understanding,** as He realized we were all working under considerable limitation and yet admired the fact that I did want the cooperation with Satellite No. 3 to continue long into the future.

In front of the congregation of The Aetherius Church in Los Angeles who attended the Sunday Service on October 16th, 1988, the Author shreds the outdated document containing the future Spiritual Push dates given to him in 1967. (See Chapter 3.) This original document had been signed by the Author, together with The Rt. Reverend Dr. Monique King (next to the Author), Reverend Dr. Charles Abrahamson and Reverend Dr. Erain Noppe (extreme left). Reverend Dr. Eleanor Abrahamson (centre) had acted as Notary Public who witnessed their signatures. Another copy of this document, kept in England, was also destroyed.

CHAPTER 5

COSMIC AWARDS

We are reprinting this Aetherius Society "Cosmic Voice," Volume 2, Issues 7 and 8, May 1981, as it is very appropriate in this present publication and will give readers a better understanding of the great happening which is described in Chapter 6:

The following Transmission was delivered by the Cosmic Master Mars Sector 6 through His Eminence Sir George King, in deep Samadhic trance, at the American Headquarters of The Aetherius Society, between 2:04 p.m. and 2:29 p.m. on Thursday, April 16th, 1981 (Earthyear 17.283):

MARS SECTOR 6:

"This is Mars Sector 6 reporting from Satellite No. 3 now in Standard Decontamination Orbit — Saturn 4.

"Satellite No. 3 will be in Magnetization Orbit of Terra as announced.

"Our rear guard combat action against powerful alien forces did result in certain superficial damage and contamination. This will be rectified and considerable improvements will be made to our protective screening, as well as our radiation devices. (Note 23.)

"At this time it is My pleasure to make the following announcements regarding promotions:

"**Nixies Zero Zero One:**
    Rank — Commander.
    Acting Rank — Vice Admiral.
    May take independent action.
    Diamond Medal Of Honour in Humanities.
    Ruby Medal Of Valour in Combat.

"Nixies Zero Zero Two:
    Rank — Commander.
    Acting Rank — Vice Admiral.
    Coordinated action.
    Electronic Comptroller.
    Sapphire Medal Of Honour in Humanities.
    Ruby Medal for Valour.

"Nixies Zero Zero Three:
    Rank — Commander.
    Acting Rank — Vice Admiral.
    Coordinated action.
    Chief Fire Control Officer.
    Diamond Medal Of Honour in Humanities.
    Ruby Medal, supplemented, for Valour.

"Nixies Zero Zero Four:
    Acting Rank — Commander.
    When necessary, a choice between true Rank — Rear Admiral, or Vice Admiral.
    Diamond Medal Of Honour in Humanities.
    Ruby Medal, supplemented, for Valour.
    Independent or coordinated action.

"Nixies Zero Zero Five:
    Rank — Commander.
    Acting Rank — Vice Admiral or Rear Admiral.
    Diamond Medal Of Honour in Surgery.
    Diamond Medal Of Honour in Humanities.
    Ruby Medal Of Honour for Valour.
    Coordinated or independent action.

"Nixies Zero Zero Six:
    In Space, Acting Rank — Commander.
    Acting Rank — Vice Admiral or Rear Admiral.
    Diamond Medal Of Honour, supplemented, for Humanities.
    Sapphire Medal Of Honour, supplemented, for Humanities.

Grieg Medal Of Honour, supplemented, for Humanities.
Ruby Medal Of Honour, with Star, supplemented, for Valour.
Action either independent or coordinated.

"George King:
The Academy Of Applied Space Sciences has made the following Awards of Merit and Honour to George King for the invention and performance of **Operation Sunbeam:**
Saturn Peace Prize for Humanities.
Venus Peace Prize for Humanities.
The Mars Sector 6 Peace Prize for Humanities.
Ruby Medal Of Honour, and two Stars, for Valour.
Rank — Classified.

"The Academy Of Applied Space Sciences has also made the following Awards:

"The Appreciation Award from Jupiter to The Aetherius Society for help in the performance of **Operation Sunbeam.**

"The Appreciation Award from Saturn for help in the performance of **Operation Sunbeam.**

"The Satellite No. 3 Special Award Of Merit And Compassion in Humanities for the help in the performance of **Operation Sunbeam.**

"The Mars Sector 6 Special Award Of Merit for the help and performance of **Operation Prayer Power.**

"The Galactic Award Of Recognition, with two Diamond Stars, to The Aetherius Society, for the help and performance of certain Missions.

"As well as these outstanding Awards, The Six Adepts have also been granted, by The Academy Of Applied Space Sciences, The Award Of Outstanding Meritorious Performance in Humanities for Their action in placing modules on certain Planets and for the design and successful orbit of Their Satellite.

"They have also been granted The Inter-Galactic Peace Prize for this outstanding feat.

"They have also been granted The Mars Sector 6 Prize Of Recognition Of Honour, with three Stars and four Clusters, for this Operation.

"All Adepts have also been granted The Aetherius Award For Honour, Merit And Valour, with supplements, two Stars and three Clusters, in recognition for Their outstanding deeds, both for humanity and in combat for humanity.

"Nixies Zero Zero Three has also been awarded The Saturn Meritorious Medal Of Honour, Valour And Outstanding Ability, with two Stars and three Clusters, for His work in the dangerous fields of combat for and on behalf of humanities.

"The launching and operation of the Satellite by The Adepts was indeed a very significant and very helpful move in that, We will, in future, be able, at times, to use this Satellite as a reflective element for Energies radiated by Satellite No. 3. We can also use this Satellite to supplement the Energies radiated by Satellite No. 3 during a terrestrial Magnetization Orbit, with Energies coming directly from certain Planets without any loss, space-warp or conditioning through Space.

"**Hence the promotions and high Awards given to The Six Adepts for one of the most significant moves ever made in terrestrial history, and indeed, as far as Terra is concerned, in the history of this Solar System.**

"This Transmission was delivered by Mars Sector 6, from Satellite No. 3, in Standard Orbit — Saturn 4.

"This Transmission was delivered with the authority of The Perfects Of Saturn.

"All Transmissions are now discontinued."

The Cosmic Transmission you have just read is one of the most unusual Transmissions ever received from Cosmic Sources since the first Contact in May 1954. The Being Who delivered this Cosmic Transmission has been known, in the past, for His impersonal, logical declarations of Truth; in fact, so much so that this could quite well be the first time, throughout His years of communication with Earth, that He ever mentioned The Aetherius Society by name.

On September 18th, 1977 (Earthyear 14.73), the Cosmic Master Mars Sector 6 stated that The Academy Of Applied Space Sciences had recognized the outstanding combat action of Adept Nixies Zero Zero One in a manoeuvre which The Master Aetherius has referred to many times as the "falling leaf." This is a very complex manoeuvre, demanding full concentration and split-second timing, so that the combat craft can be placed into a strategic position against an antagonist without that antagonist being able to predetermine its final position.

In the same Transmission, the Cosmic Master Mars Sector 6 announced that Adept Nixies Zero Zero Two had also been honoured for His invention of electronically propelling thought-energies through Space, which had the ability to adhere to almost any surface they were sent against. These balls of golden-coloured energy would burst, causing large golden flames to seem to burn very fiercely. This "golden fire" was harmless from a physical point of view, but had a disrupting effect psychologically on any antagonist as they did not know the "golden fire" was mainly a psychological weapon of defence.

The Cosmic Master Mars Sector 6 announced that these two designs became a part of the essential training for all Combat Commanders, as well as Missionaries, in the Solar System. This Transmission was never published because of reasons of security. No details as to the award of Honours appeared in that 1977 Transmission.

And then, right out of the blue as far as we are concerned, came this impressive list of Awards to The Adepts, our Founder-President and The Aetherius Society.

There is no doubt that the Cosmic Master Mars Sector 6 is indeed one of the greatest Astro-Metaphysicians Who has ever communicated with Earth. We feel that this Transmission was given at exactly the right time in order to bring into being stupendous magical power which would help all parties concerned, as well as have its far-reaching influence into many far corners of the Earth. Any Cosmic Master capable of taking charge of The Cosmic Initiation Of Earth is also capable of a manipulation of magical powers beyond our comprehension. (Note 24.)

It is not the intention, in this Issue of the Journal, to even attempt to give a line-by-line breakdown of this Transmission. However, a few ideas to give our readers a better understanding and deeper appreciation of some of these Awards are considered essential.

You will notice that The Adepts Nixies Zero Zero One, Nixies Zero Zero Four, Nixies Zero Zero Five and Nixies Zero Zero Six are Those Who are allowed to take: "Coordinated or independent action," while Adepts Nixies Zero Zero Two and Nixies Zero Zero Three are confined to: "Coordinated action." The meaning behind this is obvious. In this case, "independent action" would mean that these Adepts would be allowed, in either combat or a rescue mission, to suddenly assume Their Acting Rank — that of "Vice Admiral" or "Rear Admiral," whichever the case may be — and take action on Their own, apart from any action taken by the Fleet to which They may be attached, should the situation demand such a decision. Adepts Nixies Zero Zero Two and Nixies Zero Zero Three, because of Their specialities as "Electronic Comptroller" and "Chief Fire Control Officer" respectively, would not be able to pilot a craft and attend to these duties at the same time. This one statement alone is, in itself, an outstanding honour paid to The Adepts and a recognition of Their superb talents.

Regarding the Awards, such as: "Diamond Medal Of Honour in Humanities," received by all The Adepts, with the exception of Nixies Zero Zero Two, we feel that this is probably some device worn or carried by The Adepts. The Diamond, or as in the case of Nixies Zero Zero Two, the Sapphire, would contain a complete history of the reasons as to why the Award was given. For instance, it would be a recorded crystal which could be tied into a computer to be de-coded, no doubt giving a complete picturization of the series of events which warranted this Award being given, undoubtedly in a minimum of four dimensions — showing a third dimensional sequence with a description in sound.

The benefit of such a very practical Award is obvious. The recipient could visit any advanced System in the Galaxy, which belonged to The Galactic Confederation, and could prove His identity and accomplishments, if such proof was necessary, in order to perform a Mission or series of Missions. His skill would be recognizable immediately, even to non-humanoid forms who were intelligent enough to be able to de-code the crystal. If they did not have this coefficient of intelligence and electronic ability, then it is very doubtful that The Adept in question would ask them for their assistance, because such people would probably be useless in any complex undertaking. You would not ask an Aborigine to assist in the piloting of a terrestrial space-shuttle — neither would The Adepts seek help in a complex undertaking from inhabitants of a world who were vastly inferior in intelligence. You may, of course, seek help in the performance of less complex Missions from such a people, as indeed has been done with The Aetherius Society in many Missions we have performed; but the reference previously made is to a highly-complex Mission, such as Space combat or Space rescue, for instance.

The "Ruby Medal For Valour" would be the same, having read-out capabilities encoded within the Ruby crystal. It is also within the realms of probability that these crystals are charged with certain vital Life Forces to help the concentration and physical abilities of the recipient.

Coming on now to the reference to George King, you will see that he was given several outstanding Peace Prizes for his invention of **Operation Sunbeam,** which is easily understandable. As all our readers know, **Operation Sunbeam** was invented in 1966 as a practical way to represent mankind so that token Spiritual Energies could be given back to The Logos Of Terra Herself in recognition of Her compassion for *allowing* terrestrials to exist and be re-born on Her surface throughout the countless centuries. This is probably the first time in the history of this Planet that such a concerted attempt as **Operation Sunbeam** has ever been devised and used for this most essential of all purposes. Because of what it stands for, **Operation Sunbeam** must be man's finest:

DEMONSTRATED PRAYER OF THANKFULNESS TO GOD,

for in comparison with this, other Prayers are puny indeed!

Therefore, it is little wonder that George King received the tremendously high honour of the Award of "The Saturn Peace Prize for Humanities," "The Venus Peace Prize for Humanities," "The Mars Sector 6 Peace Prize for Humanities" and the "Ruby Medal Of Honour, and two Stars, for Valour."

Any Member who has attended the numerous lectures throughout the years on **Operation Starlight,** or attended the Seminar called, "Battle on Carnedd Llywelyn," will not be in any way surprised that our Founder-President received, from Cosmic Sources, the "Ruby Medal Of Honour, and two Stars, for Valour." His Eminence has demonstrated, in a very practical way, his high bravery factor on many occasions during his life, from rescuing lives under heavy bombardment in Britain during the war, to facing perilous blizzards on remote mountain-tops, high winds and huge storms in a small boat, to standing face-to-face against dark and evil forces — **and all these grave risks were taken for the benefit of others.**

The last sentence in the Awards column under the name of George King, given by the Cosmic Master Mars Sector 6, namely: "Rank — Classified," will cause much speculation throughout The Aetherius Society. We realize that some of this speculation will be based on insufficient evidence — but probably not all of it . . . . . !

The Cosmic Master obviously had a good reason for making this statement — probably another aspect of the magic which was generated by the Holy Transmission.

To continue with our brief examination of this unusual Transmission, the Cosmic Master Mars Sector 6 made the following statements:

"The Academy Of Applied Space Sciences has also made the following Awards:

"The Appreciation Award from Jupiter to The Aetherius Society for help in the performance of **Operation Sunbeam.**

"The Appreciation Award from Saturn for help in the performance of **Operation Sunbeam.**

"The Satellite No. 3 Special Award Of Merit And Compassion in Humanities for the help in the performance of **Operation Sunbeam.**

"The Mars Sector 6 Special Award Of Merit for the help and performance of **Operation Prayer Power.**

"The Galactic Award Of Recognition, with two Diamond Stars, to The Aetherius Society for the help and performance of certain Missions."

There is no doubt that The Aetherius Society deserved these Awards of high honour or they would not have been given. But we should all remember exactly where this Declaration places us. Because of the active nature of The Aetherius Society, which spends most of its time, effort and money on the performance of purely public service Missions, it has always been a responsibility to become an active Member. Even though these Awards were given for the deeds that we have already performed, the very fact that they were given adds to our future responsibilities.

If a Knighthood is bestowed upon anyone, it is generally because of the good deeds he has performed in the past; but because of the high honour of the Knighthood, the recipient **should behave in a more exemplary manner than he did before he received it!**

The same rules apply to The Aetherius Society after the Declaration stating that these outstanding Honours were bestowed upon us.

We have crawled from the valley up to the plateau of Service, which has been officially recognized, not only by Masters in this Solar System, but even beyond that. The higher one climbs up the ladder of Evolution, the greater the fall if the climber is not

fully aware of every step he takes. This plateau, created by our hard work for humanity and recognized by a Cosmic Declaration, gives us two choices to make:
1. To stay where we are without making any further attempts to progress even further;
2. To be so inspired that we are determined to make even further progression along the Spiritual Path of Evolution.

There is no doubt which determination we will make.

We will try our very best to do even more in the future than we have done in the past and thus be lifted upwards again to even a higher plateau than that upon which we now stand.

We think that it is correct to say that few, if any other Church of our size in the world, have done more for humanity than has The Aetherius Society.

We are extremely fortunate that we have been put in the position which we are in, mainly because we have been chosen by The Cosmic Masters Themselves to perform a series of extremely beneficial Missions, all of which have been geared to help humanity in dozens of different ways.

We have also been fortunate indeed to have been given the opportunity to work under the God-inspired guidance of our Spiritual Master, who has taught and led us into the realms of truly dedicated Service to God and to humanity.

There is no doubt that the greatest magic on this Planet is created by those whose every deed is done in the Name of Almighty God. This outlook brings strength and power way above the norm to all those who make such dedication in their hearts and Souls.

This dedication is the Path to accomplishment in all honourable fields of endeavour — **it is the Path to Spiritual Glory!**

If, in the future, everyone who belongs to or works for The Aetherius Society remembers that they are an essential part of a House of Almighty God; that every deed they do is performed, not for any individual or even a small collection of individuals, but in some degree or another for the benefit of all men and in the Name of Almighty God, then no power on this Planet can halt our most Holy progress.

All the secrets of Yoga, of metaphysics or occultism — call these sciences what you wish — are explained by those few short sentences. The very essence of Gnani Yoga — the Yoga of Wisdom — can be explained thus:

God is the Universal Creative Simple.

There is nothing except this Divine Creative Principle; neither has there ever been; neither, not even in the concept of the Greatest of the Great, will there ever be.

There are but degrees of the Evolution of this Divine Creative Principle, but these degrees of Evolution are not outside of It but are contained within Its all-encompassing Divine Form.

These are the concepts which set men free.

These are the concepts which, if really taken to the heart of every Member and sympathizer of The Aetherius Society, can propel us into a most glorious future; for if you really meditate upon this Wisdom, you will see that there is nought outside of it.

That which contains the Whole must be the Whole.

We feel that one great aspect of the Magic of the Cosmic Master Mars Sector 6, by making these announcements as He did, when He did, was to bring us back to this basic appreciation and concept of complete dedication to Almighty God; and if the Magic does not do anything else, for The Adepts, The Spiritual Hierarchy Of Earth and The Aetherius Society, then it is still a most glorious thing.

As an active Religious and scientific Society, we now stand duly honoured and we intend to live up to these Honours in every way humanly possible to us.

As Members of the very active Aetherius Society, we have been given the opportunities; we have been shown the way to put these opportunities into active manifestation for humanity, which we have all helped to do in one degree or another. We have been duly honoured for our tireless efforts and now we stand on the verge of even greater accomplishments — a truly Holy and noble position indeed.

SATELLITE USED DURING SPIRITUAL PUSH

In March 1980, one of the most significant moves in the history of the Planet Earth was made by The Six Adepts, operating in Their Full Interplanetary Aspects, with all Their knowledge and skill concentrated into individual bodies of Consciousness. Four physical modules, capable of relaying Spiritual Energies on command by remote control, were set up on Saturn, Jupiter, Venus and Neptune.

Later, on January 23rd, 1981 (Earthyear 17.200), a Satellite was put into orbit of the Planet Earth by The Adepts. (Note 25.) This Satellite has the capability, when activated in the correct manner, to receive Energies directly from each of these modules and either:

1. Store these Energies for future use; or
2. Act as a reception and radiation platform for these Energies, dependent upon the cosmotronic commands received by the computerized brain governing the function of the Satellite.

The main reason for the action upon the part of The Adepts for this truly gigantic task, was to make Spiritual Energies — pure, unadulterated and unconditioned — from these four Planets, available to the Energy release for **Operation Sunbeam.**

The Masters from Gotha, Who have made Themselves responsible for the Spiritual Energy collection for **Operation Sunbeam,** would then be able to use these ultra-pure and balancing Holy Energies in Their radiation, directly to The Logos of this Planet. This would be possible, not only through Aetherius Society Spiritual Energy Radiators connected with **Operation Sunbeam,** but also through the Spiritual Energy Radiators operated by The Spiritual Hierarchy of this Earth.

But the cosmotronic complex had another function, which was soon discovered by the Controllers of Satellite No. 3. In His famous Transmission on April 16th, 1981 (Earthyear 17.283) (full text appears in this Chapter), the Cosmic Master Mars Sector 6 made this statement:

"We can also use this Satellite to supplement the Energies radiated by Satellite No. 3 during a terrestrial Magnetization Orbit, with Energies coming directly from certain Planets, without any loss, space-warp or conditioning through Space."

The Spiritual Energy Radiator in the American Headquarters, upon command of the Controllers of Satellite No. 3, was run for two extra hours at the end of the first Spiritual Push in 1981.

The first extra hour, on Saturday, May 23rd, 1981 (Earthyear 17.320), was run between 2:00 p.m. and 3:00 p.m. (Pacific Daylight Time). The second extra hour, on Saturday, May 23rd, 1981, was run between 3:00 p.m. and 4:00 p.m.

On Monday, May 25th, 1981 (Earthyear 17.322), starting at 11:50 a.m. until 11:57 a.m., the following message was received:

"Mars Sector 8—Special Advisor S2.

"Satellite No. 3 collected and radiated Energies through the Satellite recently put into orbit by The Six Adepts, during these two extra hours.

"The first hour, Energies were radiated directly from the Planet Venus using the Satellite as a collector apparatus. During the second hour, Energies were collected from Jupiter in the same manner.

"These specialized Energies were not wholly conveyed through your radiation apparatus, but directly to Levels Three, Five and Six in both cases.

"However, .001 percent of these specialized Energies were conveyed to Level One through your apparatus.

"During the last hour of the Magnetization Period, the Spiritual Energies radiated were as normal.

"Our thanks to the valiant effort of The Six Adepts for placing the necessary modules and putting Their Satellite into a correct orbit of Terra, is hereby conveyed.

"Go with Divinity's Blessings.

"Mars Sector 8—Special Advisor S2."

And thus another highly significant move in the history of Earth was brought about!

At the end of the first Spiritual Push since The Adepts launched Their Satellite, the Controllers of Satellite No. 3 took advantage of its unusual capabilities by actually supplementing the Spiritual Energies radiated to different Levels of life on Earth, by tuning into its Energy release.

A milestone in the annals of astro-metaphysics!

Although most of the Energies manipulated by Satellite No. 3 during these two hours of Special Power Manipulation were radiated directly to life forms on Levels Three, Five and Six, .001 percent (as you can read in the Mental Transmission from Mars Sector 8—Special Advisor S2) was conveyed through the apparatus in the American Headquarters which was ordered to be operated during these times.

As far as we know, another gigantic milestone in the history of any organization on Earth!

The move, which took years of planning, scientific knowledge and compassion for a backward race, of setting the modules and putting the Satellite into orbit by those Saviours of mankind, The Six Adepts, has already begun to pay dividends of the highest Spiritual nature. These Holy Energies, used by great Astro-Metaphysicians, manipulated with a skill and knowledge borne from ancient experience, will bring about a most essential balance to the forces of nature upon which all of us are so completely dependent.

The Masters from Gotha have also used the Spiritual Energies from The Adepts' Satellite in many Phases of **Operation Sunbeam.**

Where long journeys, of hundreds of millions of miles, were necessary in the past for The Masters from Gotha to collect Spiritual Energies from near to the surface of an individual Planet, this effort is no longer necessary. At a certain distance from Earth — invisible, silent in its relentless orbit around this green Planet — the Satellite is moving through cold Space, ready at any time to be keyed into active service as a sophisticated receiving centre. The Masters from Gotha, with Their superior Space abilities, are able to orbit, in tandem, with this magnificent device and collect helpful Energies from any one of the four Planets, or even all of them together, with which the Satellite is in tune.

Little wonder, is it not, that The Six Adepts received some of the highest Awards it was possible for the Solar System and the Galaxy to give to any Life Form?

That The Adepts should even trouble Themselves to expend years of work and effort on a race as backward as that which inhabits this world, may seem strange on the face of it; but then, is not so strange when we all realize that They did this because They are much nearer to God than any of us, and therefore capable of Compassion, the depth of which we can only theorize upon.

This article is reprinted from "Cosmic Voice," Volume 2, Issues 7 and 8, May 1981.

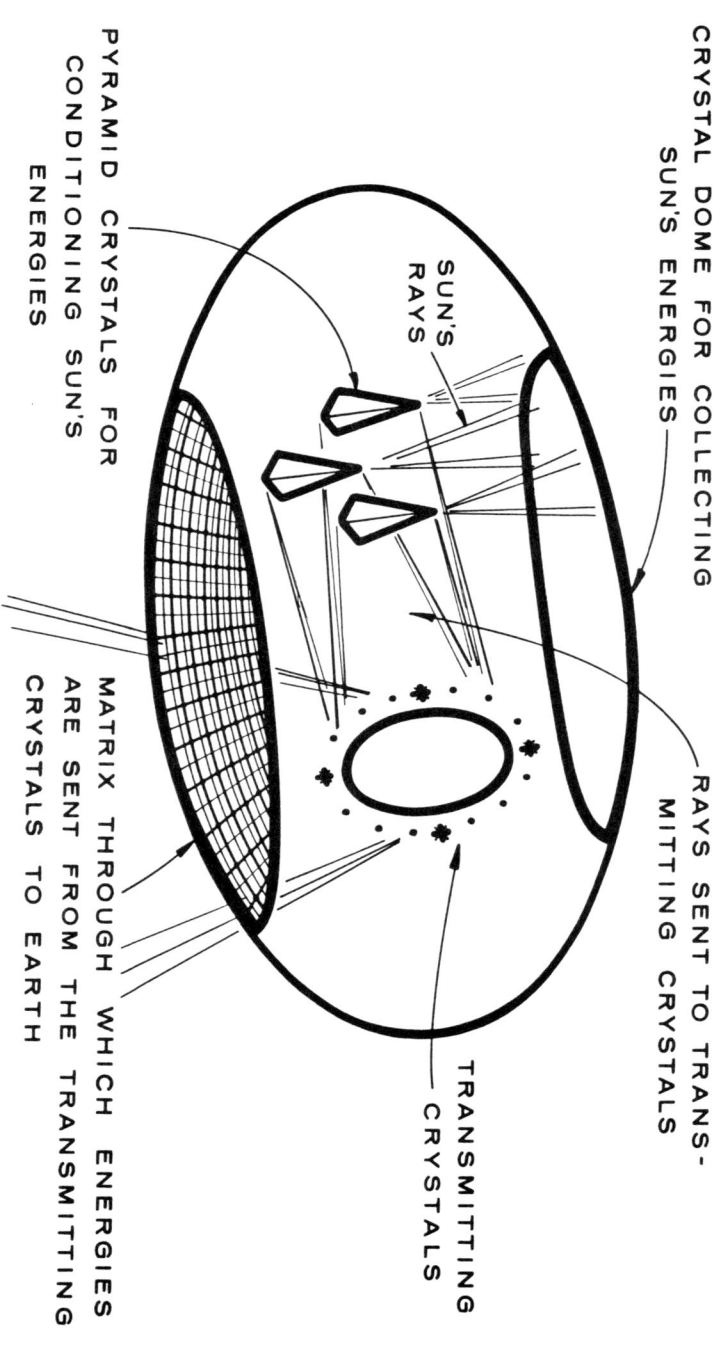

CHAPTER 6

AMAZING HAPPENING ON LAST HOUR OF SPIRITUAL PUSH

December 10th, 1988 (Earthyear 25.156)

Throughout the years, we have sent out our Prayer Power Energy from our **Operation Prayer Power** Batteries on a once-a-week basis, from both the European and American Headquarters, during every Spiritual Push. (Note 26.) However, during the last Spiritual Push of 1988, starting on November 4th and ending on December 10th, I decided to stop the Prayer Power releases from our American Headquarters because I had already been given the future Spiritual Push dates from the Karmic Lord Mars Sector 6. As you have already read, this was brought about in a Mental Transmission on October 11th.

My idea at the time was to send all four discharges of Prayer Power Energy out together in dedication to Mars Sector 6 for the tremendous help He had given to us with the Spiritual Push dates and also answering other questions which came up during those Mental Transmissions.

It became known through Cosmic Intelligence sources, that there were big changes due to take place in the near future, although these changes were, for the most part, strictly classified. However, it was known to the Few that The Five Adepts would be invited to Satellite No. 3 during the last hour of its orbit at the end of the last Spiritual Push this year on December 10th.

Satellite No. 3 comes into orbit at 12 midnight Greenwich Mean Time at the beginning of a Spiritual Push and leaves at 12 midnight Greenwich Mean Time at the end of a Spiritual Push, for other places. To invite The Five Adepts, officially, to visit Satellite No. 3 during the last hour of orbit this year on December 10th, caused many eyebrows to be raised in speculation.

What a perfect time, I thought, to make the Prayer Power discharge, just prior to this most unusual happening. So, after carefully planning out the discharge sequence, I decided to start the Operation at 1:15 p.m. Pacific Standard Time and end the sequence at 2:45 p.m. Pacific Standard Time, which still gave the Spiritual Energy Radiator Operators 15 minutes to take off the Prayer Power Battery and set up the machine for the usual last hour run in Los Angeles.

Before this happened, I contacted Mars Sector 6 and told Him about the Operation which was due to start. He was very pleased about this. He sent His Blessing to our Members who put the Prayer Energy into the Batteries to be used.

Little did Primary Terrestrial Mental Channel realize, when he **first** made the decision, at the beginning of the last Spiritual Push on November 4th, to dedicate this discharge to Mars Sector 6, that this would be performed just prior to another unique happening taking place 1,550 miles above the surface of Earth on the Command Bridge of Satellite No. 3!

Those Adepts Who live in Fourth Aspect bodies on Earth, Adepts Nixies Zero Zero One, Nixies Zero Zero Two and Nixies Zero Zero Three, must have been extremely impatient waiting for the time to come. This meant a projection from the human body to the Satellite. (Note 27.) Adepts Nixies Zero Zero Four and Nixies Zero Zero Five were in a better position because They had no encumbrance of a base physical structure and could easily, with permission, project into the Satellite.

Just after 2:30 p.m. Pacific Standard Time on December 10th, The Three Adepts began Their preparation. They were informed that there would be no danger attached to this projection as the main aspect of Their consciousness would be *escorted* from Their physical bodies and *escorted* back again. This must have been a great relief to Them, although escorted or not, They would have accepted the invitation anyway.

At approximately 2:45 p.m. (10:45 p.m. Greenwich Mean Time), They entered Satellite No. 3 and a stunning yet gorgeous sight met Their eyes.

Immediately They came into Satellite No. 3, They passed through a small room and down a corridor in which different coloured beams of Energy bathed Them. They were in a most sophisticated matter transportation device, in which the projected consciousness from Earth was amalgamated together with Their Higher Aspects. (Note 28.)

When They came to the end of the corridor, the Five of Them stood out in **Full Aspect** and in full uniform, together with Their numerous medals which They had been awarded previously by the Planetary Confederation of this Solar System.

This must have been a beautiful sight to behold!

The uniforms were pale blue in colour, decorated with gold rings and epaulets depicting Their rank.

This time, as the occasion was very formal, They all adopted Their full rank, that of Vice Admiral.

After this magical change, They were invited onto the Bridge of Satellite No. 3 to meet another most pleasant surprise, for on the Bridge there were several Masters of very high Spiritual and physical rank.

There was One of The Perfects Of Saturn — a Lord Of Karma.

There was One of The Protectors Of The Ineffable Flame Of The Planet Terra — a Lord Of Karma.

There was an Aspect of Mars Sector 6 — a Lord Of Karma.

There was an Aspect of The Master Aetherius. We do not know exactly Who The Master Aetherius is yet, except that He is an Advisor to The Karmic Hierarchy. (Note 29.)

Nixies Zero Zero Nine was also there observing, but standing in the background.

There was a Representative from the Planet Jupiter, Who has communicated many times through Primary Terrestrial Mental Channel, especially in the past. (Note 30.)

There were Others there as well.

All of Those mentioned were in humanoid forms, but there were some Who were not in humanoid forms and possibly came from other parts of this Galaxy. Some of these non-humanoids were extremely beautiful and exotic to the eye. There were not only men present but women as well. Some of the Ladies Who were in humanoid form were truly beautiful, as judged by any female standard anywhere.

Just off the Bridge and away from the large viewing screens, there were Others, dressed not in formal uniforms but in a type of one-piece garment, both the men and the women. Some wore marks on Their shoulders, possibly depicting a position. They, too, greeted The Adepts when They stepped onto the Bridge.

Altogether, the atmosphere was soft, gentle, very joyful, yet at the same time — serious. It appeared that all the Beings Who were there and Those Who worked on Satellite No. 3, did so because They wanted to. It is known that all engaged on Satellite No. 3 are volunteers, because They **want** to be so engaged in this Spiritual task of helping those who are not as highly evolved as Themselves.

There was discipline, but it was self-imposed discipline by the Operators Who wished to impose it upon Themselves.

There was no need for any discipline from another source; advice, help, learning — yes, but not what we would call discipline. It made The Adepts feel that, with the help of Cosmic Masters of this calibre, you can do almost anything which the Karmic Law will allow. (Note 31.)

The Adepts were invited to take control of the Satellite and pilot this Holy Vessel throughout its last orbit.

Nixies Zero Zero One stepped up to a huge control console, filled with rows of different coloured buttons which were internally illuminated. He started to make His calculations but before He could do this, a Perfect from Saturn, after gaining the mental permission from Mars Sector 6, walked up to the panel, moved His hands across it and the console slid neatly away out of sight!

Into its place came another set of controls.

It is known that Nixies Zero Zero One is one of the greatest combat Pilots in this Solar System, especially in Full Aspect. It is also known that He is a little choosey about His control systems and cannot do His best with masses of buttons. So a control system which had been previously built, exactly to the specification of Nixies Zero Zero One on numerous dangerous Missions, had been re-built again in Satellite No. 3!

Here we have a tough combat Pilot, One Who is not easily surprised at anything — but this did surprise Him, much to the delight of the rest of the Occupants on the Bridge!

He then sat down and reached for the controls. They fit exactly, obviously made to measure for a large, Full Aspect Being.

The rest of The Adepts turned to Their respective duties and were proud to be given the great honour, during such a formal ceremony as this, of navigating the wonderful floating Temple — Satellite No. 3.

Adept Nixies Zero Zero One took His position behind the main console and at the controls.

Adept Nixies Zero Zero Two was working the computer systems.

Adept Nixies Zero Zero Three, being a Fire Control Officer, was busily engaged in screened telepathic conversation with another Operator from Satellite No. 3, asking serious questions about the conflict in which Satellite No. 3 had been engaged in 1981 with alien vessels.

Adept Nixies Zero Zero Four was busy at the consoles, as was Adept Nixies Zero Zero Five, taking control of the Spiritual Energy radiation to Earth.

It was just about then that Mars Sector 6 made an announcement which went throughout the Vessel.

He stated that this was the last orbit of the present Satellite No. 3 around Terra!

Next year, this Satellite would be replaced by a slightly larger Vessel of ultra-modern design. Satellite No. 3, which has been operating so regularly around the Planet Earth and other inhabited worlds, was going in for a refit. The Spacecraft would then go back into service in another part of the System, probably outside of this Solar System.

Mars Sector 6 also gave Those aboard to understand that the

replacement Satellite would be a little larger than the present one. Satellite No. 3, as we have known it, was 7,920 feet long. The other replacement Satellite would be slightly larger, as Mars Sector 6 called it — 12,000 feet long.

You may like to realize that the largest ship in the world in 1987 was an oil tanker called "The Seaways Giant," and it was only 1,504 feet long. By Cosmic standards, neither of these Satellites is large; however, much larger than anything capable of movement we have on the surface of this Earth.

It was also discovered that the main Spiritual Energy collection and distribution unit in the new Satellite would be smaller than it was on this one — however, **over 100 times more powerful.** (Note 32.)

It was made known, quite definitely, by the Karmic Lord Mars Sector 6, Who is in charge of the Satellite fleet, that He did not wish the new Satellite to be called any other name except "Satellite No. 3." Not "The New Satellite No. 3" or "Satellite No. 3-2" — but just plain "Satellite No. 3."

Everybody agreed with that, including The Adepts.

This formal Gathering was brought together to give The Adepts a chance to pilot Satellite No. 3, for the last hour of a Spiritual Push, around the Planet Earth, and before the wonderful Spacecraft was taken into service elsewhere. They were truly thankful for the wonderful, thoughtful Being Who had brought this Cosmic Operation together.

Although The Adepts have earned many medals (see previous Chapter), this plan was possibly one of the best compliments which could have been paid to Them. This Cosmic Plan gave Them full recognition, in a formal manner, not only for what They have done in the past in the manipulation of Spiritual Energy for and on behalf of **all** of you, but recognition also of what They have accomplished, in fierce combat, again, for and on behalf of **all** life streams on the Planet Earth. (Note 33.)

Those very important Persons on the Bridge did not hesitate to extol the virtues of The Five, Who had accomplished so much for so many with so little.

It was unfortunate that Adept Nixies Zero Zero Six, The Lord Babaji, could not be there because He was engaged in Spiritual Energy release to the victims of the recent earthquake affecting Russian Armenia and Turkey. Adept Nixies Zero Zero Seven and Adept Nixies Zero Zero Eight were not present either because They were assisting those injured in this catastrophe.

In the course of Their orbit, The Adepts detected, through Their sensors, an object which had an invisibility screen around it. This object was soon verified as the Satellite which had been put up by The Adepts in 1981. (Note 34.) Everybody was very excited by seeing this, including The Adepts, Who had actually put it there, as They did not have such a good view of it when it was initially launched as They gained from Satellite No. 3 on the large viewing screen, with thousands of times magnification.

Mars Sector 6 informed Them that The Operators from Satellite No. 3 had used Spiritual Energy from this Satellite several times in Their Spiritual Energy radiation to Earth, as They were doing on this last orbit. On the orders of the Karmic Lord and Controller of Satellite No. 3, Their sensors were receiving Spiritual Energy from the Planets Jupiter and Venus at this time, collected by the Satellite.

The Spiritual Energies transmitted through this Satellite, when correctly coded, from Saturn, Jupiter, Venus and Neptune, or any combination of these Planets, came through without any space-warp or interference whatsoever. The Operators from Satellite No. 3 could bet on their purity, even though They occasionally did have to alter the frequencies, either up or down the range, depending on their destination.

Everybody on board was duly happy about this and if it was possible for the atmosphere of joy to arise — it did so.

The Medals of Honour worn by The Adepts were replicas of the originals and much smaller, because they were straight medals and did not include a full recording system within them. They did, however, include very pure gems, which possibly were made by technicians through the amalgamation of atoms and molecules. They were flawless. Some of them were positioned in mounts of pure gold which had been hardened by a certain process unknown to this Earth. Some were mounted in a metal somewhat similar to platinum. Some even, in an amalgamation of the two metals, very carefully blended together by a technology we are incapable of at the present time.

Each of the medals carries with it a specific power which actually helps the Wearer to concentrate on the task before Him. Such medals are only worn on very formal occasions and not worn in combat or active situations, such as dangerous rescue missions or decontamination missions; but the originals of these medals are worn for identification purposes, as you have already read. However, they certainly added to the glamour and spectacle of this really formal Cosmic Gathering.

All this time, Satellite No. 3 was proceeding at a specified velocity and was protected by screens of invisibility. These screens reflect all photon bombardment and absorb all terrestrial tracking devices, such as radar, so that They could not be detected in Their orbit. Satellite No. 3 has always adopted this procedure to avoid interference with the Spiritual Energies They radiate, some of which are very subtle. This Spiritual Energy is radiated to all those people on Earth who, whether they know about the Satellite or not, can use these Spiritual Energies, even in their daily lives, in their prayers — in fact, in all unselfish acts which are good and for the benefit of others.

The fact was being demonstrated during this occasion because of the earthquake. All terrestrial people who were helping with the rescue and treatment of victims in the earthquake area, would be helped and inspired, even though they did not know from whence came their extra power, inspiration and strength.

It was about then that Nixies Zero Zero Two brought onto the viewing screen the outskirts of London. A little later on, further over the suburbs of London, the instruments could pick up a faint bluish glow which was powerfully radiating at quite a good pressure.

Mars Sector 6 pointed out that it was the Spiritual Energy coming from the London Spiritual Energy Radiator at the Headquarters of The Aetherius Society.

As They came nearer, the sensors picked up the beams even

more distinctly. Not that the Spiritual Energy was settling on any part of London, but was heading out, possibly to other parts of the world, guided by the advanced sensors on Satellite No. 3.

When directly over the Headquarters — it was dark then, approximately 11:30 p.m. Greenwich Mean Time — the London Spiritual Energy Radiator was about half-way through the last hour of Operation in cooperation with Satellite No. 3. The emanations from the Spiritual Energy Radiator could be seen even more plainly — beautiful, glowing, yet very subtle, invisible to the human terrestrial eye.

They lit a Spiritual Fire over the dark city.

A guiding Light in the darkness.

A beautiful, glowing light, probing, moving, helping to uplift those who, anywhere in the world, could use such Holy Power.

It was then that Mars Sector 6 turned around to Adept Nixies Zero Zero One to convey His deepest thanks to His Eminence for designing and having manufactured these Spiritual Energy Radiators, which had, with the help of Satellite No. 3, done so much for so many. He said:

"Thank His Eminence very much, from Me and All of Us here, for making this decisive step forward in the Spiritual sciences. Let him know that We All appreciate his genius and also the dedicated Staff Members who operate these machines faithfully and have done so throughout the years."

This telepathic message went throughout the Spacecraft and the air was electrified by other messages of greeting and agreement with this.

Adept Nixies Zero Zero One noted the request and stated that this would be arranged.

Satellite No. 3 continued on its prearranged orbit, passing over other countries of the world, but always as the Spacecraft did so were the wonderful, uplifting, inspiring and healing Energies sent to mankind. It seems such a crying shame that most of the inhabitants of these countries did not even begin to use this Holy Power offered freely to them.

Throughout the years, The Aetherius Society has gone out of

its way to inform hundreds of thousands of non-Members, through the media, about the action of Satellite No. 3. We are stating this just so the reader appreciates the fact that, not only do Members of The Aetherius Society know about this floating Temple in the Heavens, but hundreds of thousands more who are not Members or who have not expressed any interest in our organization.

Many other happenings took place on Satellite No. 3 during that exciting last hour, but these cannot be reported.

At exactly 12 midnight Greenwich Mean Time, the Satellite came to a halt and after further Blessings of Goodwill were exchanged by The Cosmic Beings on the Bridge with The Adepts, They reluctantly left each Other's company.

As previously arranged, The Three Adepts were escorted back into Their physical structures again, thereby avoiding the dangers which surround all forms of projection from the human body.

They arrived back in Their human bodies on Earth at approximately 10 minutes past 4 p.m. Pacific Standard Time, which is 10 minutes past 12 midnight Greenwich Mean Time.

The Adepts were, naturally, sad to leave; and sentimental as well about the fact that this was the last orbit, in this part of Space, for the original magnificent Satellite No. 3. But They could reconcile Themselves that They would undoubtedly be invited to visit the replacement Vessel when that came into orbit of the Planet Earth in 1989 — and from then, on into the future.

The very reason behind publishing this book is to give the Spiritual Push dates for the future. It was most fitting that such a happening should take place when these Spiritual Push dates are on the verge of being published, so that there will be no confusion caused in the years to come when Primary Terrestrial Mental Channel — the "Voice" — has to vacate this Planet.

It was a beautiful triumph, which put the seal forever upon what the man, George King, had accomplished and had planned so that these Cosmic Missions could be continued into the future.

CONCLUSION

After writing up the amazing happenings which took place on December 10th, 1988 (Earthyear 25.156), which are reported in Chapter 6, the typesetting department of The Aetherius Society in Los Angeles went to work with a will and set up the type for the printing department.

But for some reason, unknown to me then, I did not want the printing and publishing of this book to start then. In the meantime, several more very important Mental Transmissions were received which were published in The Aetherius Society Journal, *Cosmic Voice*. (Note 35.)

I also received a Mental Transmission from Adept Nixies Zero Zero Three which I wrote up in a booklet called *The Heather Angel Story,* which, we may say, is being received very well by our readers.

I kept coming up to Santa Barbara, where the atmosphere is quiet and peaceful, and reading over the manuscript of *Contact With A Lord Of Karma,* but still was reluctant to go any further. After all, what better last Chapter could any writer have for a book of this kind than the one I had already written? It was not that I was not satisfied — if I am ever satisfied with anything I write — with the book as it was; neither was it the fact that the report of the invitation extended to The Adepts, was given by a Lord Of Karma we know as Mars Sector 6 which is written up in Chapter 6. But I had a feeling that something else of an important nature was about to be revealed.

I was right!

The Adepts gradually started to give some hints to me — although in no way officially — about certain happenings which were taking place and had continued for some time. But still nothing on an official level.

As Primary Terrestrial Mental Channel, the man responsible for obtaining the information for the book you now have in front of you, I decided to curb my impatience — and wait.

On Tuesday, April 4th, 1989 (Earthyear 25.271), between 10:55 a.m. P.D.T. and 11:20 a.m. P.D.T., the information which I had been mentally "nibbling" at for some weeks was given officially by The Master Aetherius.

This information was truly overwhelming, especially because it was given as a result of cooperative happenings which directly reflected on *Contact With A Lord Of Karma.*

I will let you read the Mental Transmission for yourself.

COMMUNICATION WITH THE MASTER AETHERIUS REGARDING CONGRATULATORY MESSAGES FROM ALL OVER THE GALAXY

His Eminence: "This is Tuesday, April 4th, 1989 (Earthyear 25.271). The time is now 10:55 a.m. P.D.T. I am in Santa Barbara.

"This is Primary Terrestrial Mental Channel opening communication with The Master Aetherius. Please come in, Master Aetherius.

"Yes, Master Aetherius. You stated previously that You had a message for me this morning. I am ready to receive it and the information will be recorded on two tape recorders."

The Master Aetherius: "**It would appear that you have caused some problem in Planetary and Galactic circles!** The problem is not yours; it is caused by the great things which have happened to you just lately, and when the word of these happenings finally arrived in certain places, there was, shall we call it, 'a flood' of communications of congratulations for you.

"I am referring to many Operations. These messages do refer to many things. Some of them have taken years to finally reach our position in the Milky Way. But most of the messages are confined to the actions of Mars Sector 6 by giving to you and your organization the future Spiritual Push dates, which of course, refer to the Operations of Satellite No. 3 in the future.

Conclusion

"Altogether, these messages now number <u>500,000</u>!"

His Eminence: "Whew!"

The Master Aetherius: "Yes, that is correct — one-half a million messages.

"As they come from Galactic Confederation sources, We could not refuse to receive them; neither can We make an attempt to pass them on to you. Suffice to say that, because of the honour payed to yourself, Primary Terrestrial Mental Channel, by a Lord Of Karma, Mars Sector 6, these messages of congratulations are flooding in and will continue to do so for many years to come! It would not be fair to try to sum the congratulatory messages up in one message, either. However, now this information has been officially released to you, you may openly declare it."

His Eminence: "Well, thank You very much, Master Aetherius. This is quite a shock, although I did have some inkling of what was happening.

"Are each of these messages from different inhabited worlds?"

The Master Aetherius: "No, they are not. Some people from inhabited worlds have sent several different messages, depending on the communication system which they have been able to set up, and the subject referred to."

His Eminence: "Oh, I see. Out of the one-half a million messages, then, would it be correct, Master Aetherius, if I say there are some authorities of other worlds who sent as many as 20 or 30 such messages?"

The Master Aetherius: "Yes, indeed some of them have done this. Some of them have even sent up to 200 messages, depending on the situation on the source Planet or in the particular Solar System from whence these came.

"It is quite correct for you to conclude that these 500,000 messages did **NOT** come from 500,000 different inhabited worlds."

His Eminence: "Thank You very much. The whole situation is, I must say, staggering, and it is mostly because of the actions of Mars Sector 6 by trusting us with the information and our offered cooperation with Satellite No. 3 in the future.

"May I ask if some of the messages do refer to the 3,000,000 (three million) Prayer Hours which were transferred on May 22nd, 1987 (Earthyear 23.319)?" (Note 22.)

The Master Aetherius: "Yes, they do, and some of them go back as far as the start of **Operation Sunbeam,** as far as the beginning of **The Alien Mission,** and so on. They are not only confined to those two actions by Mars Sector 6, but also other actions of The Adepts and so on, throughout the years." (Note 9.)

His Eminence: "Thank You very much. I think that is all the additional information I require.

"I feel this may go very well as a Conclusion to the book in which appears the information about the future Magnetization Period dates."

The Master Aetherius: "I agree. As you understand the situation so well now, you can explain it in your own words."

His Eminence: "Yes, thank You very much, Master Aetherius, but I will use Your statements as well.

"May I listen to this tape played back to make sure I have not missed anything or recorded any information on the tape which is incorrect?"

The Master Aetherius: "You may."

His Eminence: "Thank You very much."

The tape was rewound and played back.

His Eminence: "The time now is 11:20 a.m. This is Primary Terrestrial Mental Channel to The Master Aetherius. Will You please come in?

"Thank You, Master Aetherius. I realize that I will have to explain Your information on the tape, as it is a complicated

Conclusion

subject, but did You agree with it?"

The Master Aetherius: "I did.

"I also state for the readers of this book, it can be made known that the majority of these messages of congratulations do refer directly to the action of Mars Sector 6 by giving the Magnetization Period dates and the Operation of Satellite No. 3 around the Planet Terra in the future. The senders congratulate you firstly, and also congratulate your organization for the cooperation which you will set up in the future with Satellite No. 3."

His Eminence: "Thank You very much, Master Aetherius. Have You given me permission to publish this information?"

The Master Aetherius: "You may publish it."

His Eminence: "Thank You very much. I do not know how I am going to say my thanks to all these wonderful people, no matter where they are from. But anyway, I do so, lamely in a way, because I feel so very inadequate."

The Master Aetherius: "Your thanks will undoubtedly be accepted but are not necessary.

"This is Aetherius ending communication with Primary Terrestrial Mental Channel at this time — with My Blessings."

His Eminence: "Thank You. This is Primary Terrestrial Mental Channel ending communication with The Master Aetherius, with all my Blessings and all my heartfelt thanks to You for Your deep consideration.

"End of communication.

"Time now is about 11:20 a.m. P.D.T., April 4th, 1989 (Earthyear 25.271)."

After receiving this Mental Transmission from The Master Aetherius, I was so overcome by the contents that I could not write anything further that day. In fact, to be honest, it was due to the deep compassion and personal regard for me that The

Master Aetherius finished the communication as quickly and sharply as He did. Even before the end of the communication, I was overwhelmed, but nevertheless did perform the correct sign-off ritual.

How many inhabited Systems and worlds were involved in sending such a flood of messages of congratulation, I do not know, except the number is below 500,000, as was explained in the Transmission. However, that does not matter. What does matter is the **number** of different messages.

As also explained in the Transmission, some of these messages have been years in coming because of the great distances involved, as they refer to **Operation Sunbeam,** which started on September 24th, 1966 (Earthyear 3.79). This one Operation alone, according to The Cosmic Masters, started a Galactic "snowball." (Note 36.) Because it was designed by the Author on an extremely backward Planet, other peoples, who were not performing a similar manipulation to The Logos of their Worlds, were duly impressed, as soon as they heard about it, to make a start to perform their concept of this great Mission in a very determined, cooperative manner.

Some of the messages also referred to **The Alien Mission,** which started on May 30th, 1965 (Earthyear 1.327), and ended on January 22nd, 1966 (Earthyear 2.199). These messages were probably very late in coming because of the strict cloak of secrecy which was put on **The Alien Mission** and this cloak of secrecy has not yet been lifted. However, many worlds in this Galaxy must have been aware of the alien's *outward* attack on our Solar System and must have been eager to discover the outcome.

I asked a question of The Master Aetherius: did some of the messages also include the fact that a Great Lord Of Karma, Mars Sector 6, revered throughout the Galaxy, had granted, under His Orders, **three million Prayer Hours to be transferred to Central Control for future use on this Planet.** These three million Prayer Hours had originally come through our Spiritual Energy Radiators from Satellite No. 3 throughout the years and had not been used by people on Earth. They had been reclaimed by Satellite No. 3 and later transferred to Central Control on May 22nd, 1987 (Earthyear 23.319), for emergency use. A complete and full account of this most unusual happening is given in a book I wrote called *Operation Space Power.*

For your information, up to the time this book is written, we have performed 26 Phases of **Operation Space Power II** in strict conjunction and cooperation with other Missions which have been performed, such as **Operation Sunbeam** and earthquake and hurricane relief, etc.

But this still leaves the bulk of these messages of congratulation given to myself and The Aetherius Society for being trusted by The Karmic Lord Mars Sector 6, Who fixed the Spiritual Push dates for, as you have read in this book: **"As long as it is possible for The Aetherius Society to cooperate with them."**

We are honoured among The Gods!

Bear in mind that, although we do not deserve such an honour, we have worked very hard for it, with years of Spiritual Energy Radiator cooperation during **all** the Spiritual Push dates since November 18th, 1959.

The Author would like to remind readers, as detailed in the Foreword of this book, that in 1988 alone, we sent out to mankind over **two million Prayer Hours of Spiritual Power through our Spiritual Energy Radiators** in direct cooperation with Satellite No. 3. As detailed in past Aetherius Society literature and stated by The Cosmic Masters, without our cooperation with the manning of our Spiritual Energy Radiators for thousands of man hours throughout the years, mankind on Earth would not have been offered as much Spiritual Power from Satellite No. 3 as he has been offered.

We did this without thought or hope of any payment or honour. Now it seems that we have been given a superb honour, which we all consider that we do not deserve. However, our considerations do not count. What does count is the fact that The Master Aetherius revealed to us information regarding what must have been a "post office nightmare," congratulating us for our valiant work, day after day, year after year, and our determination to help impoverished or stricken life streams on the Planet Terra.

There is no organization on the physical planes of Earth which has even attempted to do what The Aetherius Society has done, under the direction of the Founder/President — never mind succeeded at it!

We are talking here not about some vague psychic dreams, or little power circles, some of whom make outlandish claims. We are talking about the **cooperation,** through specially designed equipment, with a **carefully-built Cosmic Satellite,** specially designed to offer Spiritual Power to the people on this Planet, other Planets in the Solar System, and even to the far ends of this Galaxy!

The reader would do well to remember this.

So, we are now prepared to go forward into the future and, not only perform several other Spiritual Missions, such as **Operation Sunbeam,** but also the most important task of all on Earth — the cooperation with Satellite No. 3 when the Holy Spacecraft comes into orbit of this Earth. This Mission is called **Operation Space Power.**

Because of our outstanding dedication to the greatest Cause of all, The Masters have given us the dates of the Operation of Satellite No. 3 for the next 1,000 terrene years. It is now up to us in The Aetherius Society to make sure that we do not let down the God-like trust that The Lords Of Karma have given to us.

Although this is true, the dates of the future Magnetization Periods, or Spiritual Pushes as we call them, are published in this book to also let people have this knowledge who, in the past, have had no contact with The Aetherius Society, so that they may cooperate as well, in their own chosen Religious fashion, with the beautiful, uplifting, healing Spiritual Powers which are offered to **all life streams on Earth** when this Satellite is in orbit.

If you are wise, all of you will take advantage of this help offered to you by The Lords Of Karma and The Cosmic Masters — and start a new beginning!

VERY IMPORTANT
AUTHOR'S NOTES

NOTE 1.   Read *You Are Responsible!*, Chapter 1, for details by the Author of the Command given to him in May 1954.

NOTE 2.   Study of the profound Teachings delivered throughout the years by the Cosmic Master Mars Sector 6, is highly recommended to all New Age students.

See the following books: *The Nine Freedoms; The Day The Gods Came; You Are Responsible!; Wisdom of the Planets; Life on the Planets; Cosmic Voice, Volume 1; Cosmic Voice,* Issues 22 through 26; *Join Your Ship; A Cosmic Message of Divine Opportunity.*

The following Metacassettes® contain Transmissions from the Lord Of Karma Mars Sector 6, recorded as they were delivered: Metacassette® No. MC-9, *Power Transmissions for Members;* Metacassette® No. MC-10, *Watcher in the Night;* Metacassette® No. MC-12, *Operation Prayer Power — A Spiritual Dream Come True;* Metacassette® No. MC-14, *Ye Are Gods;* Metacassette® No. MC-15, *From Freewill to Freedom;* Metacassette® No. MC-16, *Action is Essential;* Metacassette® No. MC-17, *Fight Ye the Evil;* Metacassette® No. MC-18, *Be Sane Ye Men.*

NOTE 3.   For information on the Operation of Satellite No. 3 and Aetherius Society cooperation with it, study *Operation Space Power — The Solution to the Spiritual Energy Crisis;* Chapter 4 of *The Nine Freedoms; The Day The Gods Came; Operation Sunbeam — God's Magic in Action* and *Cosmic Voice, Volume 1,* pages 32-35 and 73-79.

NOTE 4.   Read *You Are Responsible!*, Chapter 1, for an account of the Command delivered by The Cosmic Master Aetherius to the Author in 1954, which established him as "Primary Terrestrial Mental Channel."

NOTE 5. The Author has been responsible, throughout the years, for designing and manufacturing the most advanced astro-metaphysical equipment in existence on the physical planes of Earth. For an understanding of the capabilities and immense significance of the equipment used in cooperation with Satellite No. 3, study *Operation Space Power — The Solution to the Spiritual Energy Crisis; The Five Temples of God; The Age of Aetherius;* and *Operation Sunbeam — God's Magic in Action.*

NOTE 6. **Operation Space Power** is a Cosmic Mission performed in cooperation with Satellite No. 3, in which thousands of Prayer Hours of pure, uplifting Spiritual Energy are sent to mankind from Satellite No. 3 through the two Spiritual Energy Radiators of The Aetherius Society. For full details of this Mission, study *Operation Space Power — The Solution to the Spiritual Energy Crisis.*

NOTE 7. Since 1955, as a result of the contact between the Author and The Cosmic Masters, mankind has been informed of the operation of Satellite No. 3 which orbits Earth for specified periods each year known as "Magnetization Periods" or "Spiritual Pushes." During these times, Spiritual Energies are radiated from Satellite No. 3 to individuals and groups on Earth who are performing unselfish Service, which results in the enhancement of all their Spiritual action by a factor of 3,000 times. For further information, study Chapter 4 of *The Nine Freedoms* and *Cosmic Voice, Volume 1.*

NOTE 8. The dates of the future Spiritual Pushes on Earth for 1,000 years were recorded onto an official document which was duly witnessed and notarized. This document was kept sealed in a vault since that time, to be opened and acted upon after Primary Terrestrial Mental Channel had left Earth.

After the latest information regarding the Spiritual Push dates from Mars Sector 6, Who we now know is a Lord Of Karma, this document was put through the office shredder. This significant happening took place in front of the congregation of The Aetherius Society Church in Hollywood after a Sunday Service on October 16th, 1988 (Earthyear 25.101). A similar document was taken from the vault in London and this was physically burned by The Rt. Rev. Richard Lawrence, a Director, in front of five witnesses, including one other Director and the Treasurer of the European Headquarters, on October 20th, 1988 (Earthyear 25.105).

The original dates given in 1967, just prior to **Operation Karmalight,** do not really differ a great deal from the latest dates given.

NOTE 9.   **Operation Karmalight** was one of the major Missions performed by The Adepts for the protection of life on Earth from the power of evil in the lower astral realms, or "hells." This Operation was carried out between October 1967 and February 1969 and is briefly recorded in *The Aetherius Society Newsletter* of those years and the book *The Three Saviours Are Here!*

The Adepts are highly advanced extra-terrestrial Intelligences resident upon Earth, Who are dedicated to the protection and salvation of life on this Planet. Three of Them were born into the life cycle of this Earth and were subsequently joined by Two more Adepts Who, while also in Fourth Aspect, do not inhabit terrestrial physical bodies and reside mainly on the subtle realms. The Sixth Adept is The Lord Babaji, Spiritual and Political Head of The Great White Brotherhood, Who has resided on Earth for thousands of years in His Ascended Body.

For information on the heroic actions of these wonderful Beings, study of the following material is recommended. For Their Missions of protection against evil: *The Three Saviours Are Here!* (also available on Metacassette®

No. MC-25); *The Atomic Mission; Destruction of the Temple of Death/Rescue in Space;* and Cassette No. C-55, *The Men Who Won Operation Karmalight For You.* For Their actions on the higher Spiritual planes, read *Operation Space Magic — The Cosmic Connection* and *Eternal Recognition of Operation Sunbeam.*

NOTE 10. **Operation Sunbeam** is a Cosmic Mission originally conceived and designed by the Author, in which Spiritual Energies, originally intended for the use of mankind, are directed through specialized equipment into certain Psychic Centres of Earth as a token repayment of the immense energy debt owed by mankind to The Logos Of Earth. Because of the vast Karmic implications of **Operation Sunbeam,** it has been declared by Cosmic Sources to be an integral part of the Cosmic Plan for world salvation and enlightenment.

Further understanding of this Mission can be gained by a study of the following Aetherius Society publications: Cassette No. C-54, *Operation Sunbeam;* Metacassette® No. MC-2, *Operation Sunbeam Inspires The Galaxy;* and Metacassette® No. MC-19, *Gotha Speaks to Earth.* Also read *Operation Sunbeam — God's Magic in Action* and *Eternal Recognition of Operation Sunbeam.*

The history of this Mission has also been recorded in *The Aetherius Society Newsletter* and the Journal *Cosmic Voice.* Details are available from the publishers, The Aetherius Society.

NOTE 11. The Spiritual Energy Radiators were designed for **Operation Sunbeam.** Before the invention of **Operation Sunbeam** and the equipment which went with it, we had two very outdated Spiritual Energy Radiators, one in London and one in Los Angeles. His Eminence designed a Spiritual Energy Radiator as a portable, in-the-field unit for the performance of **Operation Sunbeam.** This design was made up by the craftsmen on the Staff of the American

Headquarters and it was used successfully in the first few Phases of **Operation Sunbeam**. A copy of this machine was made by the craftsmen in the American Headquarters and shipped to England. Later, never content to rest on his laurels, His Eminence designed completely different equipment for **Operation Sunbeam.**

As the old Spiritual Energy Radiators had been used by Satellite No. 3 during each Spiritual Push for release of Spiritual Energies to the world, the new machines were put into operation to replace them. These proved to be so effective that since March 1st, 1969 (Earthyear 5.237), in America, and June 7th, 1971 (Earthyear 7.335), in England, they have been in constant use for the **minimum of three hours** per day during every Spiritual Push.

For further information regarding the Karmic effects of the Spiritual Energy Radiators, read *Operation Space Power — The Solution to the Spiritual Energy Crisis* and regarding **Operation Sunbeam,** read *Operation Sunbeam — God's Magic in Action.*

NOTE 12. The Tactical Teams form part of The Aetherius Society Special Missions Task Force, an elite corps of skilled and dedicated Staff Members who assist in the correct performance of the Cosmic Missions undertaken by the Society under the direction of the Author as Commander-in-Chief.

NOTE 13. The title "Nixies," followed by a number, has been used throughout the years by The Cosmic Masters as an identification in both Their mental and trance communications. This is actually an Interplanetary Confederation identification code. It does not give away the identity of the Adept or Operative in question but is still used to identify the Person being communicated with or the Person making a communication.

As near as we can arrive at the meaning in English, it is an Adept and/or One Who has, throughout the years, performed invaluable and sometimes immeasurable Service to others, whether in this Solar System or beyond. The title does not infer that the Operative identified by such is alive in a physical body, on this or any other inhabited world.

NOTE 14. In September 1988, a fierce hurricane, given the name of "Gilbert," and registering the lowest barometric pressure ever recorded in the Western Hemisphere, swept through Jamaica causing much devastation, and then moved into the Gulf of Mexico, threatening further severe damage along the coast of Texas and north-eastern Mexico. The intervention of Higher Forces, together with an **Operation Prayer Power** release from The Aetherius Society, considerably lessened the power and destructive impact of the hurricane on life and property in that region. See *Cosmic Voice,* Volume 10, Issues 1 - 4, January/February, 1989.

NOTE 15. Adepts Nixies Zero Zero One, Nixies Zero Zero Two and Nixies Zero Zero Three were born on Earth in terrestrial bodies in order to accomplish very specialized Missions. As per The Master Aetherius in *The Five Temples of God,* this degree of Karmic help in the affairs of terrestrial man is not allowable in future. However, Adepts Nixies Zero Zero Seven, Nixies Zero Zero Eight and Nixies Zero Zero Nine will be active on the etheric realms of Earth, but like Adepts Nixies Zero Zero Four and Nixies Zero Zero Five, They will not have to suffer the tremendous limitations by living in terrestrial physical bodies.

NOTE 16. The "Karmic complexities of Terra" are the result of man's wrong thought and action throughout the centuries which have activated the Karmic Law, for the human race as a whole, in its negative phase. This, in turn, limits the extent to which more highly evolved Intelligences may intervene in terrestrial affairs to protect mankind from painful and destructive consequences of his individual and collective wrong-doing. Only when mankind learns to use his freewill in positive, constructive ways, in harmony with Divine Law, will the Great Ones be able to intervene more extensively to help him in all ways.

For a greater understanding of the Law of Karma, study of the following material by the Author, a world-renowned expert on this subject, is recommended: *Karma and Reincarnation;* Chapter 9 of *The Twelve Blessings* (as delivered through the Author by The Master Jesus); *The Nine Freedoms; You Are Responsible!; The Day The Gods Came; The Three Saviours Are Here!; The Five Temple of God; Operation Sunbeam — God's Magic in Action.*

Also, listen to the following cassettes: Cassette No. C-14, *The Spiritual Energy Crisis;* Cassette No. C-15, *Karma and Reincarnation;* Cassette No. C-20, *The Cosmic Plan;* and Cassette No. C-31, *If I Could Choose.*

NOTE 17. Listen to Cassette No. C-72, *A Physical Space Contact with a Master from Gotha* and Metacassette® No. MC-19, *Gotha Speaks to Earth,* which contain valuable Spiritual lessons and explain the presence on Earth of advanced Intelligences from the System of Gotha in order to help in **Operation Sunbeam.** These Masters play a vital role in this Mission by transmitting high frequency Spiritual Energy through The Aetherius Society apparatus to The Logos Of Earth.

On March 5th, 1989 (Earthyear 25.241), following a recommendation from the Author and The Adepts, The Masters from Gotha were invited to become full Members of the Interplanetary Confederation and upon Initiation, adopted the Title of Adepts Nixies Zero Zero Ten, Nixies Zero Zero Eleven and Nixies Zero Zero Twelve. A full report by the Author is contained in *Cosmic Voice,* Volume 10, Issues 7 and 8, March 1989.

NOTE 18. Although Mars Sector 6 has always communicated through His Eminence Sir George King under this name, in a Mental Transmission delivered by His Excellency The Master Aetherius between 9:45 — 10:15 a.m. on September 3rd, 1988 (Earthyear 25.58), His Eminence was given permission to reveal the staggering information that Mars Sector 6 had been invited to join The Karmic Hierarchy and had accepted this Honour. **Mars Sector 6 is now a Lord Of Karma.** Hence His Eminence's doubt as to what he should call this Cosmic Lord. The information release regarding this Being's elevation is published in *Cosmic Voice,* Volume 9, Special Edition No. 4, Issue 16, September 1988.

NOTE 19. **The Saturn Mission,** which started in Scotland in September 1981, is a special Operation devised by The Lords Of Saturn Who assigned the Author to be Their Chief of Operations on Terra. During this Mission, Spiritual Energies are released over a Psychic Centre of Earth to intermingle with the natural Energies radiating from that Psychic Centre, and are sent to the Devic Kingdom so that they will help to bring about a stabilization of natural conditions on Earth.

The full results of **The Saturn Mission** are unknown; however, one of the massive side results of this Mission is that, for every complete Phase performed, at least 90,000 people are saved from death or severe mutilation by natural catastrophe. At the completion of Phase 22 in November 1988, the number of people saved through this Mission was more than 2,000,000 (two million).

The history of this Mission, together with evidence of its miraculous results, has been recorded in the Journal *Cosmic Voice.* Details are obtainable from the publishers, The Aetherius Society.

NOTE 20. The Great White Brotherhood of Ascended Masters constitutes The Spiritual Hierarchy Of Earth and plays a vital role on this Planet by carrying the Spiritual Light for humanity, thereby helping to protect mankind from the repercussions of his negative Karmic pattern.

For a deeper understanding of The Spiritual Hierarchy Of Earth, study Cassette No. C-23, *The Great White Brotherhood — The Spiritual Hierarchy of Ascended Masters;* also the booklets: *My Contact with The Great White Brotherhood; A Special Assignment;* and *The Festival of 'Carrying The Light'*.

NOTE 21. **Operation Prayer Power,** a Cosmic Mission designed by the Author, is the most potent terrestrial mass healing tool ever devised for the use and benefit of ordinary man. In this Mission, Prayer Energy invoked by dedicated people is stored in Spiritual Energy Batteries which can be released, at any time, through the Spiritual Energy Radiators and directed to any part of the world to alleviate suffering in times of disaster.

For a greater understanding of this Mission, study of the following cassettes is recommended: Cassette No. C-52, *Operation Prayer Power;* Metacassette® No. MC-12, *Operation Prayer Power — A Spiritual Dream Come True;* Metacassette® No. MC-13, *Important Declaration of Truth to Terra;* and Metacassette® No. MC-21, *The Inauguration of Operation Prayer Power on Level Four.*

The history of this Mission has also been recorded in *The Aetherius Society Newsletter* and the Journal *Cosmic Voice.* Details are obtainable from the publishers, The Aetherius Society.

For information on how to participate in this on-going Mission, contact your nearest Headquarters or Branch of The Aetherius Society and read the pamphlet *Operation Prayer Power — A Spiritual Dream Come True,* obtainable free of charge.

NOTE 22. **Operation Space Power II** is the name given to an aspect of the Mission **Operation Space Power,** in which that portion of Spiritual Energies radiated through the Spiritual Energy Radiators from Satellite No. 3 during

"Magnetization Periods" throughout the years and not used by mankind, was recalled back into the Satellite and subsequently transferred to Central Control where it is held as "Credit Energy" for further use on Earth. The amount of Spiritual Energy originally set aside as "credit" was 3,000,000 (three million) Prayer Hours and was given in deference to the Author at whose discretion, with the permission of Central Control, it is released. Although some of the Energy has already been used since it was transferred to Central Control in May 1987, because of the high rate of accumulation of Spiritual Energy, there is now over 4,000,000 (four million) Prayer Hours in the "Credit Energy Account.".

Read *Operation Space Power — The Solution to the Spiritual Energy Crisis* and *Cosmic Voice,* Volume 9, Issues 13-14, August 1988.

NOTE 23. See *Cosmic Voice,* Volume 2, Issue 6, April 1981.

NOTE 24. On July 8th, 1964, the Cosmic Lord Mars Sector 6 took charge of the most advanced astro-metaphysical Operation ever reported to mankind — The Primary Initiation Of Earth. In this Operation, performed by The Cosmic Masters Who comprise The Spiritual Hierarchy of the Solar System, streams of Divine Initiating Energies were directed into the very Heart of the living, breathing Goddess — Earth. The Author was privileged to be the only channel through whom the report of this stupendous event was given to mankind and this was subsequently published in his unique book *The Day The Gods Came.* This book contains the Transmission and full explanation of this Cosmic Event, with drawings to illustrate the procedure adopted by The Cosmic Masters Who performed it.

NOTE 25. Full details of this magnificent Operation are contained in the book *Operation Space Magic — The Cosmic Connection,* written by the Author who was the official annalist for this action by The Adepts. This report of the vitally important Operation must be studied by serious students in order to appreciate the complexities of the immense task.

NOTE 26. In a Transmission delivered by the Cosmic Master Mars Sector 8 through the Author on November 17th, 1977 (Earthyear 13.133), it was stated that, starting with the "Magnetization Periods" of 1978, Satellite No. 3 would cooperate with the Mission **Operation Prayer Power** by manipulating Prayer Energy released from the Prayer Power Batteries throughout each Spiritual Push. See *The Aetherius Society Newsletter,* Volume 17, Issues 1-4, January/February 1978.

Since that time, regular discharges of Prayer Energy from the **Operation Prayer Power** Batteries have been made on specific days each week during every Spiritual Push, to be manipulated by Satellite No. 3 for the benefit of the world as a whole.

NOTE 27. The state of conscious projection referred to is very dangerous and requires a high degree of Yogic skill. During such a projection, there is superconscious awareness while the intelligence is outside of the physical structure, with memory of the experience after return to the body. It should be realized that this type of projection is far above the kind of involuntary, partial projection experienced during the sleep state, or occasionally by some people, in an uncontrolled manner while they are awake. As a Master of Yoga, the Author has demonstrated conscious projection many times throughout the years and further understanding of it can be gained by reading *You Are Responsible!,* pages 34-36; *The Nine Freedoms,* pages 121-122; and *Visit to The Logos Of Earth,* pages 55-58.

NOTE 28. Listen to Cassette No. C-62, *The Four Aspects of Creation,* for a better understanding of the advanced states of existence of these Cosmic Intelligences.

NOTE 29. His Excellency The Master Aetherius is a Representative of the Planet Venus to Interplanetary Parliament on the Planet Saturn. Throughout the years, He has been one of the main Cosmic Communicators through the mediumship of the Author. It was this Master Who gave the "Command" to the Author:

"Prepare yourself, you are to become the Voice of Interplanetary Parliament."

The Author was then given the position as **Primary Terrestrial Mental Channel** and shortly after, founded The Aetherius Society.

Read *You Are Responsible!* for a description of the "Command," and some of the wide-ranging and profound Wisdom The Master Aetherius has given to mankind, as well as a little personal information which He gave about Himself.

NOTE 30. In 1962, the Master known as Jupiter 92 delivered a beautiful Transmission through the Author, during a special series of Power Transmissions from the Planet Jupiter. This Operation was carried out to prevent catastrophe on Earth during a potentially dangerous configuration of Planets which occurred on February 4th and 5th, 1962. This Transmission, together with details of the Power Transmissions from Jupiter, are published in *Cosmic Voice,* Issue No. 26, July-August 1962.

More recently, on July 9th, 1988 (Earthyear 25.2), the Master Jupiter 92, Who signed Himself as "Controller, Interplanetary Confederation," was among many Cosmic Masters Who conveyed congratulations to the Author for the outstanding "Sacrifice To God" Discharges made on July 8th, 1988 (Earthyear 25.1). See *Cosmic Voice,* Volume 9, Issue 11, June-July 1988.

NOTE 31. Read *The Nine Freedoms,* delivered by the Controller of Satellite No. 3, the Cosmic Master Mars Sector 6, for a full explanation of the evolutionary advancement demonstrated by The Cosmic Masters on Satellite No. 3.

NOTE 32. Read *The Nine Freedoms,* Chapter 4 and Chapter 6, for a description of the functioning of Satellite No. 3 in the collection and radiation of Spiritual Energy.

NOTE 33. For information on the horrendous battles fought by The Adepts for the protection of all life on Earth, read *The Three Saviours Are Here!* This unique book gives the account of actions of vital importance to the salvation and future evolution of mankind, and contains information unobtainable from any other source. Also read *Destruction of the Temple of Death/Rescue in Space* and *The Atomic Mission.*

NOTE 34. Read *Operation Space Magic — The Cosmic Connection* for details of the Satellite put into orbit of Earth by The Adepts, and the placing of modules by Them on four Planets in this Solar System for the radiation of Spiritual Energies for the benefit of The Logos Of Earth and of mankind.

NOTE 35. See *Cosmic Voice,* Volume 10, Issue 5, February; and Issues 7 and 8, March 1989.

NOTE 36. Listen to Metacassette® No. MC-2, *Operation Sunbeam Inspires The Galaxy,* for the Transmission given by The Master Aetherius through the Author, reporting the Galactic repercussions of **Operation Sunbeam.**

All books, journals and cassettes recommended in these Very Important Author's Notes, are currently obtainable from the publishers, The Aetherius Society.